APPLE WATCH
(SERIES 4, 2019 EDITION)

APPLE WATCH

(SERIES 4, 2019 EDITION)

The Ultimate User Guide, How to Master Apple Watch In 2 Hours

Philip Knoll

Philip Knoll

Philip Knoll

IBSN:9781793059062

**Printed in the United States of America
Graw-Hill Publishing House**

2 Penn Plaza,

NY 10121

New York

USA

Dedication

To my parents, patty jean, James Knoll and my loving wife and son Diana, Kevin who are a constant source of love, encouragement, and positive energy.

Philip Knoll

Table of Contents

Philip Knoll

Philip Knoll

Philip Knoll

Intentionally left blank

APPLE WATCH
(SERIES 4, 2019 EDITION)

The Ultimate User Guide, How to Master Apple Watch In 2 Hours

Philip Knoll

Download these powerful books for free

today

 **Free books for buying this book.**

Philip Knoll

Chapter 1

Introduction

I Want to thank you and congratulate you for downl oading the book "**Apple watch series 4**".

This is an updated version that contains proven steps and strategies, tips and tricks on how to master Appl e watch in 2 hours. When the Apple Watch was initi ally debuted release in 2015, it wasn't exactly clear w

Apple Watch series 4

hat problems it solved or who would be its demographic group. Johnny I've the company directors admitted that during an interview with him. Apple basically knew it desired to create a super watch that would figure out what it would do after the fact. Following launch, there was a laundry list of issues that hampered the Apple Watch's abilities, relegating it to being a slow sidekick to the iPhone. It could not process much locally, offloading the majority of the work to the iPhone. Watch faces were quite limited, as were the complications that could run on them. Making the situation worse, it was slow to launch apps and Siri was less than helpful. Developers, initially excited about Watch's prospects, beg *an to flee the platform, with much pulling support in r ecent app updates.Over the past few years, Apple Wat ch hasn't seen much more than incremental spec bumps , with Apple is adding features like better water resist ance, faster processors and cellular as on where Apple Watch excelled. On the outside, the Apple watch desig n remained largely the same for three years. It's one of the most frequent questions among people looking to ge t the Apple Watch for the first time what does this sw atch really do?*

Apple Watch series 4

Have you wondered why many want to get the latest se ries 4 of Apple watch? Do you want to learn the best ways, tips and tricks so that you may utilize your watc h and maximize its efficiency? You are on the right co urse of learning the most effective ways to utilize your Apple Watch using this book. Thanks, once again, fo r downloading this book, I hope you enjoy it.

Apple watch series 4

Philip Knoll

In-depth unboxing of the series 4 Apple watch

Nevertheless, despite all this, in the time since the debut, the users defined Apple's product in search of a mar

ket, and Apple has taken note.

Everything changed with the Series 4. It easily stole the show from the iPhone XS and iPhone X'S Max during Apple's fall media event. After spending some time with the Series 4, things have started to become clear. The Apple Watch has graduated from the iPhone's sidekick to a hero all of its own.

A new face

You can't start talking about the Apple Watch Series 4 without first touching on that new display.

Apple Watch series 4

Apple has increased the size substantially over the previous models. e smaller model, now 40mm, has a 35 percent larger display than the old 38mm Watch and the largest 44mm version increased real estate by 32 percent over its 42mm predecessor.

Philip Knoll

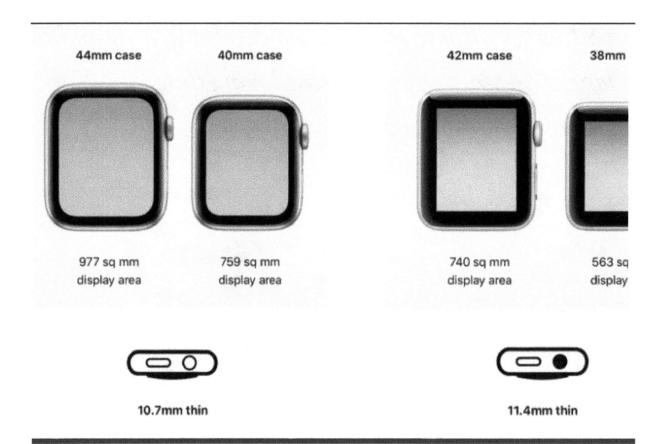

44mm case — 977 sq mm display area

40mm case — 759 sq mm display area

42mm case — 740 sq mm display area

38mm — 563 sq display

10.7mm thin

11.4mm thin

10

Apple Watch series 4

Each display now uses a low temperature polycrystalli ne oxide (LTPO) OLED display, which require a bi t less power to run than the previous generation panels. hey are also a tad thinner, which helped Apple reduce d the overall thickness of the Apple Watch. What makes these new displays really pop is a combination of other effects alongside the physical size increase. Th e bezels around the Apple Watch are significantly thin ner. They aren't nonexistent, but they are much smalle r. Apple has rounded the corners of the display that m irrors the newly rounded corners of the updated case.

The bigger the display, reduced bezels, and more round ed case create the illusion of vastly larger displays while keeping the physical size of the watch nearly identical. Going back to the Series 3, the display feels incredibly cramped. Of course, there are downsides here. Many U I elements have just expanded in size to fill the new di splay, without consideration of better use of the space. I wish Apple had tried to better utilize the new space r ather than just scaling the elements up.

There are some areas that take advantage of the real e state, such as the two new watch faces exclusive to Seri es 4. Inforgraph and Inforgraph Modular have many updated complications included rounded ones to fit the corners. Up to nine complications can fit within the inf ographic face, making them exceptionally dense. Those looking for more information out of their Apple Watch will love these new options.

Developers have already started to add support for these new complications, and it will be exciting to see what they are capable of as time moves on.

Four other watch faces have made their way to the Series 4. Vapor, liquid metal, breathe, and fire & water. We saw these four faces already with watch OS 5 on existing Apple Watches, but they were clearly designed more with the Series 4 in mind.

Instead of being relegated to a simple ring within the display, on the Series 4 they go edge to edge, filing the ent *irety of the watch face. They looked great, and even better.*

Speed

This year, the Apple Watch is running off of the S4 system-in-package. For the first time, it is a 64 bit processor that should see speeds up to twice as fast as that of the S3. The speed improvement is nice, but the S3 was already quite quick. Apple's S3 processor was a huge upgrade ofthe S2, and that means that when comparing the S3 to the S4 side by side, you do not always see a huge difference. Aple watch Series 4 is n o slouch, letting apps launch fairly quickly and makin g Siri more responsive than ever.

To go with the new S4 is the W3 wireless chip. Unfo rtunately, Series 4 is still limited to 2.4GHz, 802.11n, but it did get an upgrade to Bluetooth 5. Bluetooth 5 was included in the iPhone X, so really the Apple Watch is just playing catch up.It adds add i tional range and bandwidth, which could be useful to connect to the host iPhone, as well as when run-ning legacy apps that still handoff a lot of data from the iPhone itself.

Instead of keeping the back of the Apple Watch meta l with a composite or sapphire crystal sensor, the Series

4 has a ceramic back surrounding the sapphire covered heart rate sensor.

Health-first

After calibrating sights on the target for four iterations , Apple has zeroed on the bull's eye of what the Apple Watch should focus on this time around. First is data . They've helped conquer that by adding improved cellular connectivity, a large display, and additional watch faces and complications. Second is health, which they have bolstered with a variety of new features in watch OS 5 and on the Series 4.

Apple Watch series 4

There is a new gyroscope-accelerometer that is capable of measuring twice the dynamic range and up to 32G. This new range, coupled with the speediness of the S4 c hipset, allows measurement, sampling to happen eight t imes faster. That new improved performance lets Appl e Watch Series 4 monitor a new data point falls. App le has trained the watch on three distinct types of sudde n descent. A straight down fall, a slip, or a trip. With their motion pattern, distinct.If the watch detects any of these three, it will display an alert saying that a fall was detected, and ask if you're OK. You can swipe to call emergency services or tap a button to dismiss the al ert, recognizing that you are OK.

If no motion detected for 60 seconds, then it will auto matically be notified emergency services and your locati on sent to your emergency contact alongside a message s aying you may be hurt.

This feature is off by default unless your age is above 6 5, but it can turn easily be on within settings.

Heart monitoring was also bolstered in Apple watch series 4 this year. Precedent Apple Watch mode ls have been able to monitor your heart rate throughout the day for elevated rates, and watch OS 5 now allow s it to watch out for low rates as well. On Series 4, the re is support for identifying atrial fibrillation and tak- ing an ECG. Both of these features are missing at lau nch, though will be showing up with the watch OS 5.1 later this fall at least in the United States.

Physical feedback

Apple watch embraced its physical element of the old version, realizing the significance of the original design. This can be seen in no better way than investigative the taptic engine housed inside the Apple Watch.

This electromagnetic linear actuator provides the delightful tapping feeling on the back of your wrist at whatever time a notification comes in.

Philip Knoll

It takes up an amazingly large portion of the Apple Watch's cavity, space that could have gone towards a bigger battery or a thinner design. Instead of removing that, Apple in its place has doubled down with the Series 4.

Whenever, using that same taptic engine, Apple is intelligent to simulate physical notches on the Digital Crown. As you rotate the wheel, it should feel rough like it is clicked, making all the experience the better.

When our team tested this, we were a little underwhelmed at the expected effect. It still feels like the taptic engine, and not essentially like physical notches. At the s ame time, however, it does add to the capacity to contro l the watch without looking.

The effect is only present whenever in an actual scrolla ble situation. This is fantastically similar to the glass t rackpad on the MacBook. As soon as the machine is off, a press on the trackpad registers no physical feedba ck, on the other hand when on, it feels like a slick. A pple has used a comparable process here. When the wa tch is off, or on a screen that is powerless to scroll, rotating the crown does nothing — and feels like nothing.

Philip Knoll

Perfecting the watch experience

Apple has gone a long way of perfecting the user experience with series 4. The display is larger, the Digital Crown feels more exact, health functionality h as been significantly improved above every other fitness tracker, and they've managed to do this all while main taining the same battery life. With normal routine use, Apple watch fourth generation wearable is still capabl e of "all day battery life" which amounts to be about 1 8 hours. That's the same hours given for the previous g eneration. Unexpectedly, the battery itself is actually s *maller, but optimizations in hardware and software have allowed, permitted it to have the same lifespan.*

This series comes with both cellular, GPS models and 16GB of onboard storage, meaning that more audio files can be saved locally. The speakers on the Series 4 were overhauled. There was a significant difference not just in volume, but quality when receiving calls and using Walkie-Talkie.

The speakers have been even more crucial in recent years as Siri gets more responsive and accomplished, watch OS debuts new features such as Walkie Talkie,

Philip Knoll

and you can answer group Facetime calls right from yo ur wrist. The speaker besides being louder, the microp hone was moved to the opposite side, which might help reduce echoes when taking calls, depending on which h and you wear the smart watch.

Chapter 2

WHAT WE ARE EXPECTING ON APPLE WATCH SERIES 5

Apple's watch series is one of the best selling on the earth and prettify wrists all over the world - although it's not all perfect. The Apple Watch series 4 is the company's most well-designed device.

Philip Knoll

The Apple Watch series 4 saw come with an ECG monitor — even though that's not a feature that has been activated all over the world yet — as well as fall detection function and a refreshed design that ensures existing straps can be used while offering more screen space.So why are we talking about the Apple Watch 5? At the moment, we're expecting it to be called the Apple Watch Series 5, and below we've collected all of the rumors we've seen so far. There aren't many rumors yet though, so more importantly you'll find a variety of improvements we'd like to see on the next Apple Watch 5 from Apple.

Apple Watch series 4

Apple Watch 5 release date and price

We don't actually know the specific time when the Apple Watch 5 will launch, but we can make an educated guess. It's worthwhile buying the Apple Watch 4 right now as the device is only a couple of months old and we don't expect to see an update from the Apple company until September 2019.

Generally speaking, the Apple Watch 3 and Apple Watch 4 were both introduced in September of their respective years, so we'd expect the company to follow a similar costume for its next device.

Regularly Apple introduces devices and then releases them 10 days later as well, so once whenever you've heard about the Apple Watch 5 it perhaps won't be long until you can purchase one.

But, When it comes to devising price, we have no genuine reason to believe the price is set to increase from the RRP of the Apple Watch 4. That watch started at $399 / £399 / AU$599 for the smallest GPS version and $429 / £429 / AU$649 for the larger one 44mm one.

If you wish for mobile internet, you'll be able to buy the smaller watch for $499 / £499 / AU$749 and

Apple Watch series 4

$529 / £529 / AU$799 for the larger watch. There probably some fluctuation when it comes to the Apple Watch 5 prices, but this is the clearest pointer of how much it'll cost you when it launches.

Apple Watch 5 news and rumors

Presently, we've yet to hear much about the Apple Watch 5, but information may give us a hint at what we'll see. The first important statement comes from trusted Apple analyst Ming-Chi Kuo, who has stated that the company may be set to introduce a "new ceramic casing design" on at least one model.

Philip Knoll

Ming-Chi Kuo also believes Apple will innovate and bring support for the ECG monitor to more countries with the Apple Watch 5. Probably, that may also be a software upgrade for the Apple Watch series 4 - as well as a new means to charge your watch.

He believes Apple will take up two-way wireless charging on its next generation of smartphones, which would mean you'd be able to place your Apple Watch on the back of an iPhone 11 and charge it up using your phone's battery.

Apple Watch series 4

In another place, it has been reported that Apple is working on a sleep tracking features, so the Apple Watch 5 might finally be capable to track your sleep without you needing to download any third-party app.

known that much of the hardware should already be in place, it's likely that sleep tracking will also come to older models as a software update. On the other hand, the report says that the feature should arrive by 2020 so we might not see it until the Apple Watch series 6.

Another report has also claimed that Apple will be looking to Japan company to make OLED panels for the Apple Watch series 5. That's not likely to have any effect on the end product, but it's also fascinating to see the company is already preparing its manufacturing deals ready for this year's device.

An official document filed by Apple shows a system that can monitors chemicals in the air to 'smell', which could track a body odor or sense air quality where you're exercising. Little is known about the Apple Watch 5. But there are consistent rumors surface each year with Apple patenting round screens and a various type of other technologies, but at the time of writing this book, we have no reason to believe these are true for this device.

Apple Watch 5: what we want to see

A new watch from Apple optimistically means some meaningful new innovation. The Apple Watch series 4 was a big change for the wearable line, but we're hoping for even more on the next-generation of Apple Watch. Here's what we're in suspense for:

1. Improved battery life

The previous generation of Apple Watch doesn't have the worst battery life for a smartwatch, but neither does it have the best one.

Philip Knoll

The Apple Watch Series 4 does have the best battery life we've seen on a smart watch line from the company so far... but still we want more. Apple may be able to improve more on its processing tech more out of the battery that's already inside or the company will include a larger cell to upshot in improved battery life.

Apple may even take an essential step and include a low battery mode like we've seen on other watches, for example, the TicWatch Pro.

2. A wider selection of apps

This is amazing things that would improve the entire Apple series of wearables. We've seen major players drop support for Apple Watch plus Instagram and Slack, and we'd like to see Apple invest in getting those users back onto watchOS.

Even If it can't get the big name services, we'd like to see Apple get developers more involved in the platform to create innovative apps for the service that compete and beat Tizen and Wear OS.

3. And something special for Spotify

2018 saw the introduction of a Spotify app on Apple Watch, but it's not what everyone wanted. You can only use it to control music on other devices, meaning *you can't download albums or playlists straight to your Apple watch.*

Apple Music does allow that on the Apple Watch, so why can't the company comprise similar support for Spotify? Honestly, we'd like to see the company embrace support on its wearables such as Tidal, YouTube Music and a variety of other streaming services as well. It'd be a major step for Apple to open up like this and in return, it'd mean a lot for some users.

4. Better sleep tech

Apple Watch series 4

For Apple's sleep tracking technology isn't the best on the Apple Watch, because, we have found that it doesn't always track each night's sleep with reality accuracy. We'd like to see the company focus on improving this feature that some find important on their Apple watch.

You can buy a range of different sleep monitors that can be installed, and we'd like to see Apple embrace its top-end heart rate tracking tech to rival some of these.

5. A slightly thinner design

This 's another one we're constantly asking for, but the Apple Watch does still feel thick on your wrist. The Series 4 in 44mm does feel thinner because it's larger, but it's still a thicker device than other smart watches.

Apple may be able to trim it little down a touch further too by including smaller processing tech and possibly a new battery tech. We don't know how Apple can do it, but we'd like it to.

6. Support for Android

Here's the one on the list we're almost sure won't happen, but we're including it anyway. We'd like to

Apple Watch series 4

see the Apple Watch series 5 include support for all Android devices.

In the last five years since the initial announcement of the original Apple Watch we've always wanted this, but the company has kept compatibility limited to its own iPhone line alone.

Android Wear started later but out as a platform for those with Android phones, but a few years in the company opened it up for support with iPhone as well. That has been a major benefit for the company and at last count, over a third of its users were on iPhone.

Wouldn't that mean a gush in sales for the Apple Watch if it suddenly worked with Android devices?

Apple has made one of the best smartwatches in the world that money can buy, why not share it with everyone? It almost certainly won't happen, but we can dream.

7. Another gamechanger

You might not be able to use this feature right now, but allowing for an electrocardiogram (ECG) easily on a smartwatch is a gamechanger for everyone who's anxious about their heart health. We'd like to see

Apple Watch series 4

Apple follow that up with another feature that makes our jaws drop on the Apple Watch series 5.

That's an easy task, right? It's considered the new ECG feature on the Apple Watch series 4 is set to be embraced on a variety of competing smartwatches from other manufacturers coming in 2019 proving Apple is an innovator with this tech.

We don't know what that next thing will be, but we're always sure that the brains at Apple are already trying to come up with unique new tech. Perhaps a

Philip Knoll

device that's suitable for those who suffer from diabetes or other chronic diseases? Only time will tell.

Chapter 3

Important handling and safety information about Apple watch

My dear, you should take all the necessary precautions, failure to follow this safety information could result in fire, electric shock, injury, or damage to your Apple watch or other property. Take time and Read all the safety information in this chapter before using Apple Watch if you are a novice.

Ways to handle Apple Watch with care.

The Apple Watch cover case is made of various materials that include Apple Watch 316L stainless steel, ceramic, and sapphire crystal. The Apple Watch Sport 7000 series has aluminum, Ion-X glass that is strengthened glass, plastics.

Apple Watch Edition

It is made up of 18 karat gold, sapphire crystal, ceramic Apple Watch contains sensitive electronic machinery and can be spoiled if dropped, burned, punctured, or cr ushed. However, you should not use a damaged Apple Watch, such as one with a cracked screen, visible water intrusion, a damaged band, because it may cause injury. Keep it away from heavy exposureto dust or sand.

Repairing Apple Watch

Don't ever open the Apple Watch and don't try to repair Apple Watch yourself. The reasons are that disassembling Apple Watch may perhaps damage it, result in failure of water resistance, and may cause injury to you as well. If Apple Watch is malfunctioning or damages, contact an Apple Authorized Service Provider.

Philip Knoll

Apple Watch battery

Don't try to replace the Apple Watch battery by yours elf. You may probably damage the battery, which could cause overheating and subsequent injury. The lithium ion battery in Apple smart Watch should be serviced o nly by an authorized qualified service provider. You co uld receive a replacement Apple Watch when ordering battery service. Batteries must be recycled and disposed properly separately of household waste. You should never incinerate the battery.

Distraction sometimes may occur using Apple Watch in some circumstances may cause a dangerous situation (for instance, avoid texting while driving your car or using headphones while riding a bicycle).

Observe all rules that prohibit or restrict the use of mo bile phones or headphones (But, you may allow using h ands free options for making calls while driving).

Maps Navigation

Maps, directions, and location based apps depend on data services. These data services are subject to chan ge from time to time and may not be obtainable in all areas, resulting in maps, directions, or location based i

47

nstructions that may be unavailable, inaccurate, or inc omplete. Some map features require your Location Ser vices. Always compare the information provided by A pple Watch to your environs and defer to posted signs t o resolve any discrepancies. Do not use these services w hile doing activities that need your full attention. For a ll time comply with posted road signs and the laws and regulations in the areas where you are using Apple W atch and at all the times use your common sense.

Apple Watch series 4

How to charge Apple Watch,

To charge Apple Watch, use only the Apple Watch

Philip Knoll

Magnetic charging cable and it is the power adapter (a nd, for Apple Watch Edition, the included Apple W atch Magnetic. You may likely use third party Lightn ing cables with 5W power adapters featuring an MFi logo. It's imperative to keep Apple Watch, the Apple Watch Magnetic charging cable, and the power adapte r in a dry, well ventilated area when charging. When c harging Apple smart Watch Edition in the Apple W atch Magnetic charging case, always keep the case open . Using an Apple Watch Magnetic damaged charging cable or Apple Watch Magnetic charging case, or char ging when moisture is present, can cause fire, spark, ele ctri c shock, injury, or damage to Apple Watch or other property.

Ensure that, Apple watch and the Apple Watch Mag netic charging cable or Apple Watch Magnetic chargin g case are well dry before charging. Whenever you use t he Apple Watch Magnetic charging cable or Apple W atch Magnetic charging case to charge Apple watch, m ake sure that your USB plug inserted fully into the ad apter before you plug the adapter into a power outlet.

Philip Knoll

You should avoid charging Apple Watch in direct sun light. Moreover, remember; Don't wear your smart Watch while it is charging.

Lightning cable and connector

Lightning cable and connector should avoid prolonged skin contact with the connector when the Lightning to USB cable is plugged into a power source because it m ay cause irritation or injury. Sleeping or sitting on the Lightning connector should totally be avoided.

Protracted heat exposure of Apple Watch.

The Apple smart watch Magnetic charging cable, the Apple Watch magnetic charging case, and the power adapter complies with appropriate surface temperature standards and limits. Still, even within these limits, sustained contact with warm surfaces for long periods may cause soreness or injury. Apple S mart Watch, the Apple Watch magnetic charging cabl e, the Apple Watch Magnetic charging case, and the p ower adapter will become very warm when plugged into a power source. Use universal precaution to avoid situ ations where your skin is in prolonged contact with A pple Watch, the Apple Watch magnetic charging cable

, the Apple Watch magnetic charging case, or the power adapter for long periods when they're plugged in. For instance, while Apple smart Watch is charging or while the Apple Watch magnetic charging cable, the Apple Watch Magnetic charging case, or the power adapter is plugged into a power outlet, so that you don't sleep on them or place them under a blanket, pillow, or your body. Take extraordinary care if you have any physical condition that affects your ability to detect heat against the body. Always remove Apple smart Watch if it becomes disturbingly warm.

Listening sound at high volume

Hearing loss may result when Listening to sound at high volumes may damage your hearing. Background noise, as well as constant exposure to high volume levels, can make sounds seem quieter than they actually are. Usually, turn on audio playback and make sure the volume level before inserting a Bluetooth connected headset in your ear is within the safety level. To prevent potential hearing damage, do not listen to high volume levels for Radio frequency exposure Apple smart Watch uses radio signals to connect to wireless networks.

Philip Knoll

Radio frequency interference

You should also observe the signs and notices that pro hibit or restrict the use of electronic devices (for instant, in healthcare facilities or blasting areas). Even though Apple smart Watch, the Apple Watch magnetic char ging cable, and the Apple Watch magnetic charging ca se are better designed, tested, and manufactured to com ply with regulations governing radio frequency emission s, so all emissions from Apple Watch, the Apple Wat ch magnetic charging cable, and the Apple Watch mag netic charging case can negatively affect the function of another electronic gadget, causing them to malfunction. The best thing to do, is to unplug the Apple Watch m agnetic charging cable and the Apple Watch magnetic charging case and turn off Apple Watch or use the Ai rplane mode when the use of Apple Watch is prohibite d, like when traveling in aircraft, or when asked to do so by state authorities.

Medical device interference

Apple smart Watch contains components and radios t hat emit electromagnetic waves. Apple Watch, some of the bands, the Apple Watch magnetic charging cable, and the Apple Watch magnetic charging case enclose

57

magnets.

These electromagnetic waves and magnets may impede with pacemakers, defibrillators, and other medical devices.

Always maintain a safe distance of parting between yo ur medical device and Apple Watch, its bands, the A pple smart Watch magnetic charging cable, and the A pple Watch magnetic charging case.

The most important thing is to consult your physician and medical device company for information specific to your medical device. Urgently stop using Apple Watch , its bands, the Apple Watch magnetic charging cable, and the Apple Watch magnetic charging case if you ex pect they are interfering with your pacemaker, hearing aids, defibrillator, or any other medical device.

Apple Watch is not a medical device, but it has the he art rate sensor, and that's been included Apple Watch apps are not medical devices and are intended for fitne ss only. They are not designed for use in the clinical di agnosis of disease or other conditions, or in the cure, ea sing treatment, or prevention of medical disease.

Before starting or modifying any physical exercise program using Apple smart Watch, consult your physi cian. Be cautious and attentive while exercising. Stop e xercising immediately if you experience pain, or feel fai nt, dizzy, exhausted, or short of breath.

As a result of exercising, you assume all associated n atural risks, including any injury that may result from such activity. If you have any medical condition that yo u consider could be affected by Apple Watch (for insta nt, seizures, blackouts, eyestrain, and headaches), it's better to consult your physician prior to using Apple Watch.

Explosive atmospheres device

Charging or using Apple Watch in any area with a p otent, explosive atmosphere, such as areas where the ai r contains high levels of flammable gases, vapors, or pa rticles (like as grain, dust, or metal powders), may be hazardous. Comply with all signs and instructions.

Take note of high-consequence activities, Apple Watch is not wished for use where the failure of the device coul d lead to any loss of life, personal injury, or severe envi ronmental consequences.

Choking hazard, Some small Apple Watch bands m ay present a choking hazard to small children. Keep th ese bands away from reaching small children.

Philip Knoll

Skin sensitivity reaction

Some people may experience skin reactions to certain materials used in jewelry, watches, and other wearable items that are in prolonged contact with your skin. This may be due to allergies, environmental factors, exposure, extensive to irritants such as soap, sweat, or other causes.

You may be more liable to experience irritation from any wearable device if you have allergies and other sensitivities. If you have recognized skin sensitivities, please take special care when wearing Apple Watch. You ma

Apple Watch series 4

y be more likely to experience irritation from Apple s mart Watch if you wear it too tightly. Strip off Apple Watch periodically to let your skin to breathe.

Keeping smart Watch and the band clean and dry will surely reduce the possibility of skin irritation.
If you experience any of redness, swelling, itchiness, or any other irritation sign or discomfort on your skin, or beneath, your Apple Watch, please remove it and con sult your physician before resuming wear. Persistent us e, even after symptoms subside, may result in an increased irritation.

Philip Knoll

Nickel hypersensitivity

Apple smart Watch, particularly, the space gray Apple Watch Sport, the stainless steel portions of some Apple Watch bands, and the magnets in the watch and bands have some nickel. Nickel exposure of these materials is improbable, but customers with known nickel hypersensitivity should be attentive when wearing them until when they can determine they are not experiencing an allergic reaction.

Apple Watch, the Milanese Loop, Modern Buckle, and Leather Loop bands comprise of trace amounts of methacrylates from adhesives. Methacrylates are norma

Apple Watch series 4

lly found in many consumer products that are exposed to the skin, including adhesive bandages, however, some people may be sensitive to them, or increase sensitivities over time.

The materials used in Apple Watch and the Apple Watch bands must meet with the standards set in jewelry by the U.S. Consumer Product Safety Commission, applicable European regulations.

Philip Knoll

Chapter 4

How to get started

A quick look at Apple Watch

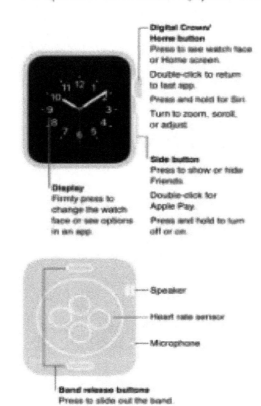

Apple Watch series 4

Your Apple watch has the capability to respond to yor

stures. If you lke to use Apple Watch and its apps it required these gestures. The pple Watch display not on

ly respon

ds to touc

h-based

gestures

alone,

such as

tapping

and

swiping

but also

useFTT)

Swipe up, down, left, or right.

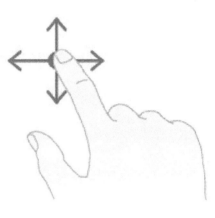

Drag.

Tap.

Firmly press the display—don't just tap.

Force Touch Technology to act in response to the small pressure of your fingertip Tap.

How to set your Watch pair with the iPhone

Toward setup Watch this book will guides you through a few simple steps to pair Apple Watch with your iPhone and make it customaries to your wish. If you have any difficulty seeing the Apple Watch or iPhone screen to set it set up and pair.

Philip Knoll

Here are the solutions, Update your iPhone to iOS sof tware version 8.2 or much later then, go to Settings> General > Software Update, which includes the travel companion Apple Watch app. After that, open the Apple Watch app on your iPhone.

Apple Watch

Apple Watch series 4

Put your Apple Watch on your wrist, press and hold the side button until you see the Apple logo displays on the screen.

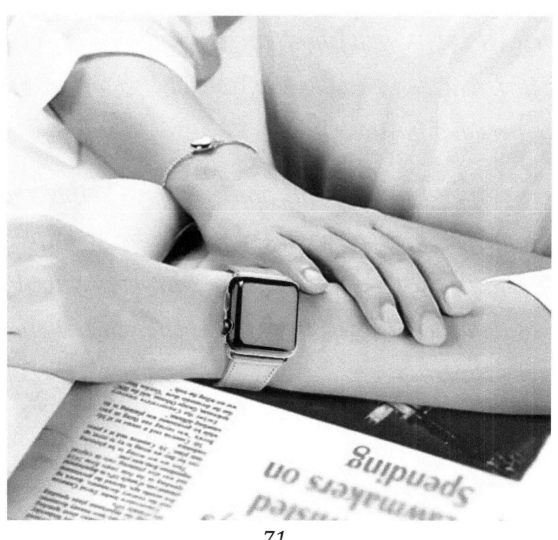

Philip Knoll

Once prompted, you should position your iPhone so that Apple Watch appears in the camera viewfinder on your iPhone screen. Strictly follow the orders on iPhone and Apple Watch to ensure the setup finish accurately. It is very important during setup session; you will select your desired language, your watch orientation, and personal passcode.

Here is another important caution before getting started; you may need to charge your Apple Watch to a battery maximum capacity before pairing it with iPhone so that you will experience any power interruption during the setup session.

Apple Watch series 4

For best performance of your Apple Watch always change or clean the watch band. Apple Watch should fit closely loosely, but comfortably on your wrist and adjust it accordingly.

Philip Knoll

Apple Watch series 4

The Status icons of you Apple Watch at the top of the screen provide information about Apple smart Watch:

From top to bottom

1. Notification: You have unread notifications.
2. Charging: Apple Watch is charging.
3. Lock: Apple Watch is locked with a passcode.
4. Do Not Disturb: Calls and alerts won't sound or light up the screen, but alarms are still in effect.
5. Airplane Mode: Wireless is turned off but non-wireless features are still available.
6. Apple watch disconnected from your iPhone: Apple Watch has lost the connection with its paired iPhone.

7.*Loading: There is wireless activity or an active process happening.*

The Apple Watch app on iPhone

The Watch app on iPhone lets you modify watch settings and options and you may set up Apple Pay for Apple Watch. It gives you access to the

App Store, that you can download and install a lot of apps for your Apple smart Watch.

Apple Watch series 4

Open your Apple Watch app. Then on iPhone, tap the Apple Watch application icon, tap My Watch to open the settings for Apple smart Watch.

Power on, wake, and unlock

How to turn power on your Apple Watch

When your Apple Watch is off, press and hold the side button on your Watch until the Apple logo displays, and you might see a black screen appear for a short time, at that moment waiting for the watch face.

Philip Knoll

Turn off Apple smart Watch.

You will be able to power off Apple Watch— then press and hold the side button until the slider disp lay, then drag it to the right of your watch.

Wake Apple Watch.

If you want to wake up Apple smart, Just lift or raise d your wrist or tap on the display. And your Apple Watch goes to sleep when you lower your wrist. You can as well wake Apple smart Watch by pressing the Digital Crown that is useful if you're not on your wrist.

But if Apple smart Watch doesn't wake when you lift up your wrist, now you must ensure that you've selected the accurate wrist and Digital Crown orientation.

Open the Settings app on your watch and make sure you're looking at the watch face, press the Digital Crown to get to the Home screen, then tap, go to General > Orientation, then ensure that Orientation is set to the wrist you wear Apple Watch on.

Wake to the watch face—or your last activity.

You can set Apple smart Watch to give you an idea about the watch face when it wakes up, or return back t

o where you were before it went to
sleep. The default setting is to wake the watch face.

Select return back to the last app you used

Open settings on your smart Watch, tap General
>Activate on Wrist Raise, and make Wrist Raise is
turn on.

Then scroll down to select opening to the last-used
app. You might also do this by means of the Apple W
atch app on iPhone: tap My Watch, go to General >
Activate on Wrist Raise, then choose Resume
Previous Activity.

Unlock Apple Watch with iPhone.

You can unlock your Apple smart Watch by putting your iPhone passcode on iPhone, open the Apple smart Watch app on iPhone, tap My Watch, tap Passcode, then tap Unlock with iPhone. Or, on Apple Watch, open Settings, scroll down, tap Passcode, then turn on Unlock with iPhone.

Remember that you can set up Your Apple Watch passcode to differ from your iPhone passcode. In fact, for more security of your gadgets, it is better to make the passcodes different.

How to enter passcode into Apple Watch

Whenever you take Apple smart Watch off your wrist or wear it very slackly, it always asks for your passco de the next time you try to use it. When the number pad displays, just tap your passcode.

To change your passcode

On Apple smart Watch, open Settings, scroll down, t ap Passcode, then tap Change Passcode and follow the step on screen prompts. Enter the at least new 4-

digit passcode, and then confirm it. Alternatively, open the Apple smart Watch app on iPhone, tap My Watch, tap Passcode, then tap Change Passcode and follow the onscreen prompts.

How to change the passcode

Enter a longer passcode.

If you wish to use a passcode longer than four digits, o pen the Apple Watch app on iPhone, tap My Watch, tap Passcode, then turn off Simple Passcode. A simpl e passcode is a 4 digit number. With this option of, yo u can set more than 4 digit passcode on your Apple smart Watch.

To turn off the passcode

Open Settings, tap Passcode, then tap Disable Passco de. Alternatively, open the Apple smart Watch app o n iPhone, tap My Watch, tap Passcode, then tap Tur n Passcode Off. Mind you, If you ever Disable your p asscode, you can no longer use Apple Pay on Apple smart Watch.

You can lock it automatically.

Turn on wrist recognition as detection to lock your watch automatically when you're not wearing it. Open the Apple smart Watch app on iPhone, tap My Watc h, tap General, and then tap Wrist Detection. When y ou turn on *Wrist Detection, you can also see the time when you raise your wrist. If you turn off Wrist Detection, you cannot also use Apple Pay.*

You can lock it manually.

Here you Press and hold the side button until the sliders display, then yank the Lock Device slider to th e right. You'll be asked to enter your Watch passcode the next time you try to use Apple Watch. You can al so put the watch into Power Reserve mode from the screen.

How to erase Apple Watch data

You may set Apple Watch to erase its data if the wro ng password is entered 10 times. This protects the cont ents of your watch if it is stolen or lost.

Open the Apple smart Watch app on iPhone, tap My Watch, tap Passcode, and then tap Erase Data.

But If you fail to remember your passcode what to do?

Just unpaired Apple Watch from its paired iPhone to delete your Apple Watch settings and passcode.

You may also reset Apple Watch and pair it once aga in with your iPhone.

How to adjust brightness, text size, sound s, and haptics

To adjust brightness. On the watch Settings app, then scroll down and tap Brightness & Text Size.

Tap a Brightness icon, then turn the Digital Crown or tap the brightness icon to adjust. Alternatively, open t he Apple Watch app on iPhone, tap My Watch, tap Brightness and Text Size, and then drag the Brightness slider.

Compose the text larger.

Open smart Watch Settings, then scroll down and tap Brightness & Text Size. Tap Text Size, then tap the letters or scroll the Digital Crown to enlarge or reduce the text size. Alternatively, open the Apple smart Watch app on iPhone, tap My Watch, tap Brightness & Text Size, and pull the Text Size slider.

How to make the text bold

On your smart watch Settings, scroll down and tap Br ightness and Text Size. Click on Bold Text. Alternat ively, open the Apple smart Watch app on iPhone, tap My Watch, tap Brightness & Text Size, and then turn on Bold Text.

Whenever you turn on bold text from any of Apple W atch or your paired iPhone, Apple Watch has to be reset to apply the change. Then tap Continue.

How to adjust Apple Watch sound

Open your smart Watch Settings, then scroll down an d tap Sounds and Haptics. Tap the volume buttons be low Ringer and Alert Sounds or tap the slider one tim e to select it, and then turn the Digital Crown to regul ate the volume. Alternatively, open the Apple smart Watch app on iPhone, tap My Watch, tap Sounds

& Haptics, then pull the Ringer and Alert Sounds slider.

Mute Apple smart Watch.

To mute, you watch just open Settings, and scroll down and tap Sounds and Haptics, then turn on Mute. Or otherwise, swipe up on the watch face, Swipe to the Settings glance, then tap the Mute button. You may also open the Apple Watch app on iPhone, tap My Watch, tap Sounds and Haptics, then turn on Mute. Apple Watch connected to its companion iPhone.

Turn on Mute. *You can swiftly mute new alert and all notification sounds by resting the palm of your ha* nd on the watch display and holding it there for at lest four seconds.

You'll be aware of a tap to confirm that mute is on. You must initially turn on the option in the Apple Watch app on iPhone. Then tap My Watch, tap   Sounds and Haptics, turn on Cover to Mute.

How to adjust haptic intensity

On your Apple smart Watch taps your wrist for certain notifications and alerts, and you can regulate the intensity of this haptics. Open Settings, then scroll down and tap Sounds & Haptics. Tap the haptic buttons below Ringer and Alert   Haptics   or   tap   the *slider once to choose it, then turn the Digital Crown to adjust the haptic intensity. Alternatively, open the Apple Watch app on iPhone, tap My Watch, tap Sounds & Haptics, then pull the Ringer and Alert Haptics slider.*

Do not Disturb is a simple way to silence Apple smart Watch.

It keeps calls and alerts with exception of alarms from making any sounds or lighting up the screen.

How to turn on do not Disturb

Swipe up on the smart watch face, swipe left or right to the Settings peek, then tap the Do Not Disturb button. Or open Settings, tap Do Not Disturb, then turn on Do Not Disturb. Whenever Do Not Disturb is on, you'll see them at the top of the screen. Tap to turn on Do Not Disturb.

To silence, both Apple Watch and iPhone

Open the Apple Watch app on iPhone, tap My Watch, and turn on Do Not Disturb > Mirror iPhone. Moreover, any time you can change Do Not Disturb on one, the other will change to match.

Philip Knoll

How to modify Apple Watch language an d orientation

If you want to change language, or your region format. Then unlock the Apple Watch app on your iPhone, tap on My Watch, then go to General > Language and Region.

Control wrists or modify the Digital Crow n orientation.

If you would like to switch wrists or rather to orient th e Digital Crown another way, just adjust the orientati on settings so that when raising your wrist will wake Apple Watch, and turning the Digital Crown moves things in the direction you look forward to.

Now open the Settings app, then go to General > Orientation. To change the settings in the Apple smar t Watch app on iPhone, then tap My Watch, then go to General> Watch Orientation.

Set orientation options on Apple Watch or in the Apple Watch app.

Philip Knoll

How to charge your Apple Watch

Make sure that you always charge Apple smart Watch h.

In a well ventilated place. Position the built in Apple Watch magnetic charging cable or Apple Watch magnetic charging case on a flat surface, then plug it into the included power adapter in Apple smart Watch pack, or you may even use a power adapter you use with your iPhone or iPad, and then plug it into an appropriate power outlet. Once using the Apple Watch magnetic charging case, always keep the case open.

Place and position the back of Apple Watch on your c harger. In such a way that the magnets on the charger line up Apple Watch properly, and you'll hear a chim e sound except if the Apple Watch is muted mode and see a charging sign on your watch face. The charging sign is red when Apple smart Watch wants power and turns green when Apple smart Watch is charging.

Checking battery power remaining

On Apple smart Watch, swipes up on the watch face, then swipe to the battery glance. You can add the batte ry indicator to several of the watch faces, plus modular, color, utility, simple, chronograph, and Mickey mouse. *With the watch face showing, firmly press the display, tap customize, and then swipe to the left until you can select individual feature locations. Here just tap a location, turn the Digital Crown to select battery, and then press the Digital Crown to exit.*

Use power reserve to stretch available power.

You can set Apple smart Watch in power reserve mode so that to save power when the battery is low. Apple smart Watch continues to keep and display time, but other apps will not be available for use. Swipe up on your watch face, swipe to the power glance

, tap power reserve, then tap Proceed. You may also press the side button until you see the slider show, and then drag it to the right.

You should take note that your Apple smart Watch automatically enters into power reserve mode if the percentage your battery charge left behind drops below 10 percent.

How to return to normal power mode

Just press and hold the side button to restart Apple smart Watch. Make sure there is sufficient charge in the battery for this to work perfectly.

Philip Knoll

Checking time for the last charge

Open the Apple smart Watch app on iPhone, tap My Watch, then go to General> Usage, where you can o utlook the Usage and Standby values.

These values, further together, give you the elapsed time since your last full charge. Below that, you can see the power reserve value.

Chapter 5

Basics of Apple Watch

Philip Knoll

How to make use and organize apps

They're all on a single Home screen, where you can organize them as you wish. To open an app your smart watch. On your watch face, press the Digital Crown to get to the Home screen, and then tap the app icon. Alternatively turn the Digital Crown to open either app is in the center of your Watch Home screen.

How to make return to the last app.

To return to the last apps is to double click the Digital Crown.

To return to the watch face

Tap the watch icon on the Home screen to return to your watch face. Alternatively, just press the Digital Crown.

Rearrange your apps.

On your Apple smart Watch, press the Digital Crow n to go to the watch home screen. Touch and hold an a pp till the apps shake to and fro and the app icons ap pear the same size and then drag the app you want to move to a new place. Press the Digital Crown when yo u're done. Alternatively, open the Apple smart Watch app on iPhone, tap My Watch, then tap App Layou

t. Touch and hold an app symbol, then drag it to a ne w place. Tap Reset to restore the original layout setting.

How to get and install apps from the App Store

Open the Apple smart Watch app on iPhone, and the n tap the App Store to find apps for your Apple Smart Watch. Buy it, download, and install apps on your iPhone. On your Apple Smart Watch, you'll not ice a message prompting you asking to install the app. Then tap Yes.

To adjust settings for installed apps

Open the Apple smart Watch app on your iPhone, tap My Watch, and scroll down to see your apps you want to adjust. Tap an app name to change its settings.

To check storage used by apps

Open the Apple smart Watch app on your iPhone, tap My Watch, then go to General > Usage. View the storage used by each app and the accessible storage left on Apple smart Watch.

Philip Knoll

How to hide an installed app in Apple Watch

On your Watch home screen, touch and hold the app icon until you view an X on the border. Then tap the X to get rid of the app from Apple smart Watch. It remains installed on your paired iPhone, unless if you remove it from there.

To display or hide installed apps

On your Apple smart Watch, open the Apple smart Watch app on iPhone, tap My Watch, scroll down to view apps you've already installed, tap the app name, and then tap Show App on Apple smart Watch.

However, *mind you, you cannot hide any apps that already in-build with your Apple smart Watch.*

How to get in touch with your friends

The site button on your Apple smart watch gives you s wift access to people you lives in touch with the most. P ress the side button, choose a friend, then call, send a message, or use Digital Touch. Add your friends to your Apple Watch.

Philip Knoll

How to add friends to Apple smart watch on iPhone

Apple Watch routinely adds up to 12 of your choice contacts from iPhone. You can amend the list of friends that appear on your Apple smart watch, open the Apple Watch app, then tap My Watch, then tap Friends. In your friends list, tap Add friend, then tap your friend in the list of contacts that appears on the screen. If your friend name isn't on the list, open the Contacts app on your iPhone and add them, subsequently try again.

To see friends on Apple smart Watch

Press the side button to see up to 12 friends contact. Turn the Digital Crown to highlight every one of your friends. Tap a friend's initials, and then select how you want to get in touch.

How to use Hand to shift between Apple Watch and iPhone

The Hand of aspect on Apple Watch and iPhone lets you move from one device to another without losing focus on what you're doing. For instances, you can simply check email on Apple smart Watch, but you may want to switch to iPhone to type an answer using the on s creen keyboard. Basically, wake iPhone, and you see a symbol in the lower left corner of the Lock screen that matches the app you're using on Apple smart Watch-for instance, Mail. Swipe up on the sign to open the same email on iPhone, and then finish your reply.

You may use Hand off with these apps: Mail, Maps, Messages, Phone, Calendar, and Remember as wellas Siri. For Hand off to work, your Apple smart Watch should be in close proximity to your iPhone.

How to turn Hand off

Open the Apple smart Watch app on your iPhone, then tap My Watch, then turn on General> Enable Handoff.

How to locate your iPhone

Misplaced your iPhone? Apple Watch can help you find out if it's nearby. Ping your iPhone. Swipe up on a watch face, swipe to the Settings glance, tap the Ping iPhone button.

If iPhone is not in range of Apple smart Watch, you can also try to find it using find My iPhone from the site called iCloud.com.

How to use your watch without pairing with iPhone

Even though, you need an iPhone to do most of the things with your smart Watch, but you can still do quite many things with Apple Watch without having an iPhone in range.

You can do the following without pairing with your iPhone

Apple Watch series 4

1. To play music from a stored playlist on Apple Watch

2. To use the watch, alarms, timers, and its stop watch

3. You can keep a trail of your activity such as stand, move, and exercise with the Activity app in the smart Watch

4. You can also track your workouts

5. To display photos from stored photo albums

6. To use Apple Pay to make purchases in online store.

Philip Knoll

Apple smart Watch uses Bluetooth wireless technology to bond to its paired iPhone and uses the iPhone for se veral wireless functions. Apple smart Watch can't con nect with new WiFi networks by itself, although it can connect to WiFi networks you've already set up on the iPhone.

If Apple smart Watch and iPhone are on the same ne twork ranges but are not connected by Bluetooth, you c an do the following on Apple Watch with no iPhone:

1. You can send and receive messages by means of iMessage

2. *And you can send and receive Digital Touch messa ges*

3.   *Using of Siri*

The function of Siri on Apple Smart Watch

The Siri on the Apple can execute tasks and deliver lots of information right on Apple smart Watch.

How to ask Siri a question

Philip Knoll

To ask a question to Seri Just raise Apple smart Watch or tap on the screen. When the Watch wakes, speak "Hey, Siri"

You can alternatively press and hold the Digital Crown on the watch until you see the listening icon at the bottom of the screen, state your request and then release the Digital Crown. To answer back to a question from Siri and continue the conversation, hold down the Digital Crown and talk. On the other hand, simply say "Hey, Siri" and your request.

Press and hold to activate Siri.

You'll discover suggestions of things you can ask Siri throughout this book -they look like this:

"What kinds of things can I ask you?"

When you fly with Apple Watch

When you are about to fly an airline, some airline might let you fly with Apple smart Watch and iPhone turned on if you put them in Airplane Mode so they can't obstruct with aircraft wave systems.

Philip Knoll

How to turn on Airplane Mode

To turn on Airplane Mode in your smart watch. Swipe up on the watch face, and a Settings glance, then tap the Airplane Mode button.

The Connected status of an airplane icon at the top of the screen changes to Disconnected. Or otherwise open t he Settings app, then tap Airplane Mode. When Air plane Mode is on, you'll see it at the top of the screen of your watch.

Apple Watch series 4

If you want to set both Apple Watch and iPhone in Airplane Mode, open the Apple Watch app on iPhone, tap My Watch, and turn on Airplane Mode > Mirror iPhone. Then, at any given time you switch to Airplane Mode on one gadget, the other will switch to match it appropriately. To turn off Airplane Mode, you ought to do it for each device separately. However, it is better to turn off Wi-Fi and Bluetooth, put the Apple smart Watch in Airplane Mode

Philip Knoll

Chapter 6

A quick look at Apple Watch

**Digital Crown/
Home button**
Press to see watch face
or Home screen.

Double-click to return
to last app.

Press and hold for Siri.

Turn to zoom, scroll,
or adjust.

Side button
Press to show or hide
Friends.

Double-click for
Apple Pay.

Press and hold to turn
off or on.

Display
Firmly press to
change the watch
face or see options
in an app.

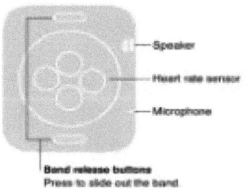

Speaker

Heart rate sensor

Microphone

Band release buttons
Press to slide out the band.

120

How to customize your watch face

You may customize your Apple smart Watch face so it looks the way you feel like and provides the functions you want. Select from different types of watc h face designs, adjust colors, facial appearance, and oth er details, then add it to your collection subsequently yo u can switch when you like the right timekeeping tools or when you'd like a change the face.

Philip Knoll

To change the watch face

With the Apple watch face showing, tightly press the display, and then swipe to see the faces in your collection. When you find the face you want, tap it. Swipe to see other watch faces. Tap to add features to your watch face.

You can add extraordinary functions. Occasionally refers as complications, to your watch face, so you can directly check something like stock prices or the weather report.

Add features to your Apple watch face.

On the watch face, firmly press the display, then tap C ustomize. Swipe to choose a feature, and then turn the Digital Crown to adjust. But on some watch faces, you have to tap a feature to pick it.

Then, press the Digital Crown to save your modificati on. Tap the face to switch to it. Turn the Digital Crown to adjust features.

Ways to add a watch face to the collection.

Gather your own collection of custom faces, even differe nt versions of the same design. When your watch face showing, tightly press the display, swipe from to the rig ht, then tap the New button (+). And swipe up and down to select designs, then tap the one you like to add . After you add it, you also can customize it.

How to delete a face from your collection

If you don't like a face much anymore? By the current watch face showing, tightly press the display, swipe to t he face that you don't feel like, then swipe it up and ta p delete. You can all the time add the watch face again later.

How advance the watch time.

If you want to set your watch time ahead? Open the Se ttings app, tap Time, tap +0 min, then turn the Digit al Crown to set the watch ahead by a great extent of 5 9 minutes. However, this setting can only change the ti me shown on the Apple watch face even though it does n't affect alarms, times in notifications, and any other times like World Clock.

Features of the Apple Watch face

Philip Knoll

Apple smart Watch consists of a different watch face, some of which you can customize. You should frequently check for software updates and the set of watch faces that follows might vary from what you see on your Apple smart Watch.

Solar system astronomy of Apple Watch

The Astronomy watch face displays the status of the solar system and the precise position of the planets, sun, and moon, and shows the day, date, and current time zone.

Tap the Moon to see its current phase.

Apple Watch series 4

Tap to see the current position of the planets in the solar system. While viewing the Earth, moon, or the solar system, turns the Digital Crown to move back or forward in time.

Chronograph

This watch face dealing with time in exact increments, like a classic analog stopwatch. A chronograph is like a stopwatch, which can be activated right from the face.

Philip Knoll

1. Adjust basic characteristics: Dial details• Face color

2. Add to the watch face: such as date

• Calendar

• Moon phase

• Sunrise and Sunset

• Weather

• Stocks

• Activity summary

• Alarm

Apple Watch series 4

• *Timer*

•*Battery charge*

• *World Clock*

Color

This watch face shows the time and any appearance
you add in your choice of bright colors.

1.Adjust basic characteristics: Dial color
2.Add the watch face: Date • Moon phase •
 Sunrise/sunset • Weather • Activity summary •
 Alarm • Timer • Stopwatch • Battery charge •
 World Clock • your monogram (displays initials

above the center; initials are taken from your Contacts information)

Mickey Mouse of Apple Watch

The Mickey Mouse provides you a fantastic view of time, and watch his foot tap of the seconds.

Add to the watch face:

1. *Date*

2. *Calendar*

3. *Moon phase*

4. *Sunrise/sunset*

5.   *Weather*

6.   *Activity summary*

7.   *Alarm*

8.   *Timer*

9.   *Stopwatch, Battery charge, and World Clock*

The Modular of Watch face

The Modular watch face has a lithe grid design that lets you add several features to give you a systematic view of your day.

1.Adjust basic characteristics: Color

2.Add the watch face: Date • Calendar • Moon phase • Sunrise/Sunset • Weather • Stocks •Activity summary • Alarm • Timer • Stopwatch • Battery charge • World Clock •Expanded view s of Calendar, Weather, Stocks, Activity, Alarm, Timer, Stopwatch, and World Clock

The Motion

The Motion of Apple smart watch face shows a beautiful animated theme such as butterflies, flowers, or jellyfish.

1.To adjust basic characteristic: The animated butterfly, flower, or jellyfish
2.Add the watch face: Date (with or without day)

Apple Watch series 4

The Simple

This small and simple, elegant Apple watch face lets you add the detail aspect of to the dial and features to the screen corners.

1. *Adjust basic uniqueness: Color of the sweep hand • Detail and numbering of the dial*
2. *Add the watch face: Date • Calendar • Moon phase • Sunrise/Sunset • Weather • Activitysum mary • Alarm • Timer • Stopwatch • Battery charge • World Clock*

Philip Knoll

The solar

This function based on your current position and time of day, the Solar watch face shows the sun's position in the sky, in additions to the day, date, and current time.

Utility

This watch face is useful and functional; you can add up to three features to display what you like to see at a glance on your watch screen.

1. Adjust basic characteristics: Color of the second hand

2. Detail and number of the dial

3. Add the watch face: Date • Calendar • Moon phase • Sunrise and Sunset • Weather • Activity

summary • Alarm • Time• Stopwatch • Battery charge • World Clock • Expanded views of all the preceding features plus Stocks

Chapter 7
The Apple watches notifications.

Swipe down on the watch face to see unread notifications.

The function of this App sends notifications to keep you informed always such as meeting invitations, messages, and exercise reminders are just a few mentions. Notifications are displayed on Apple Watch as almost immediately as they arrive. If you do not read them instantly away, they can be saved, thus you can check them later.

How to reply to live notifications

When you get a new notification. If you hear or feel a notification beep arrives, raise Apple smart Watch to view it. Turn the Digital Crown to scroll to the bottom of the notification, and then tap a button there. Alter natively, tap the app symbol in the notification to open the related app.

To dismiss a notification

Swipe down on the notification you're about reading, o r scroll to the bottom of the notification and then tap Dismiss.

How to select which notifications you like

On your iPhone, go to Settings>Notifications to identi fy which apps and events create notifications. Then, op en the Apple smart Watch app on iPhone, tap My W atch, tap Notifications, tap the app for instant, Messages, then select Mirror my iPhone. or, to select different notification settings than those on iPhone, select Custom instead.

How to silence the notifications

To silence notifications on Apple smart Watch, swipe up on the watch face, swipe to the settings glance, then tap on Silent Mode. You'll feel a tap when a notification arrives. To put off sound or tap, tap Do Not Disturb.

Philip Knoll

Keep it your Watch private.

You raise your wrist to see a notification; you get a swift summary, then details a few seconds later.

For instance, when a message arrives, you see Who it's from earlier, and then the message appears. If you want to completely stop the notification from appearing then you tap it, open the Apple Smart Watch app on iPhone, tap My Watch, tap Notifications, then turn on Notification Privacy.

How to answer the unread notifications

Seeing notifications that haven't responded to. If you d on't respond to a given notification when it arrives, it's saved in Notification Center in your Watch. A red d ot at the top of your watch face indicates you have an u nread notification. Swipe down on the face to view it. If you want to scroll the notification list, swipe up, dow n, or alternatively turn the Digital Crown.

To respond to a notification in your list. Tap the notification.

Tap a notification to respond to it.

How to clear notifications

Apple smart Watch always removes notifications from the list when you tap to read them. However, if you want to delete a notification without reading it, swipe it to the left, and then tap Clear.

Moreover, if you like to clear all notifications, tightly press the display, and then tap Clear

Chapter 8

Quick glances

T

Swipe up on
the watch face
to see glances.

Philip Knoll

To get a quick glance at the valuable information from your watch face, then you have quick access to Glances, scanable summary of an information you view mainly. Swipe up on the watch face to see glances, then swipe left or right to see different types of glances. Swipe left or right to view all glances.

Check your glances

Swipe up on your watch face to see the glance you viewed last, then swipes left or right on your Apple Watch to see other glances. Swipe down to return to the watch face. If a glance isn't enough.To open the related app, just tap the glance.

How to organize your glances

To select your glances, open the Apple smart watch app on iPhone, tap My Watch, tap Glances, and then remove or include glances. You can't remove the settings glance totally. But put them in a handy sort. Open your Apple smart watch app on iPhone, tap My Watch, tap Glances, and then pull the reorder buttons.

The timekeeping appearance of Apple smart watch, you can see the time in other cities of the world, set ala rms, use timers, and use a stopwatch. You can   also add these basics to your watch face to see them swiftly when you need.

How to check the time in other locations

The World Clock app on Apple smart Watch lets you can check the time in cities around the world. Open the app to check times at another place, or add c ities to your watch face for swift reference.

For instance, "What time is it now in New York?"

Check the time in a different city.

Apple Watch series 4

Open World Clock on your smart Watch, and then turn the Digital Crown or swipe the screen to scroll down the list.

If there is a city location whose time you'd like to see, y ou can add the world clock to your watch face and select the city name to display.

See Additional information.

To see more information about a city, together with a time of sunrise and sunset, taps the city in the World Clock list.

When you're ending, tap < in the upper left, or swipe

right to return to the city list. You can press the Digita l Crown to return to the Apple watch face.

Add any city to the World Clock. The cities you need to add on the iPhone displays in World Clock on Apple smart Watch.

Open the Clock app on iPhone, tap World Clock, and then tap the Add button (+).

Add a world clock to your watch face

You can add a world clock to quite a few watch faces, some faces give permission you add more than one. Tig htly press the display, and then tap Customize. Swipe left until you can choose individual facial features, tap the one you'd want to use for a world clock, and then t urn the Digital Crown to select a city. When you're do ne, press the Digital Crown. You may add a world clo ck to these faces:

Such as Chronograph, Color, Mickey Mouse, Modula r, Simple, and Utility.

To change city abbreviations. If you like to change a city abbreviation used on Apple smart watch, open the Apple Watch app on iPhone, tap My Watch, then g o to Clock > City Abbreviations. Tap whichever city to change its abbreviation.

How to set an alarm

To use the Alarm Clock app to play a sound or vibrate Apple smart Watch at the right time. You may also add an alarm to your watch face, thus you can see upcoming alarms at a glimpse. Moreover, open the Alarm Clock app with a tap.

"Set repeating alarm for a PM."

To add an alarm to your Watch. Open Alarm Clock, tightly press the display, then tap New +. Tap Chan *ge Time, tap AM or PM, tap the hours or minutes, turn the Digital Crown to change, and then tap Set. Tap < in the upper left to return to the alarm settings, then set repeat, label, and snooze that suit you.*

Add alarm. Set alarm time. Select options.

Set or adjust your alarm. Open Alarm Clock, and then tap the alarm in the list to modify its settings. Tap next to the alarm to turn it on or off. Moreover, tap to edit an alarm.

"Turn off 7:30 alarm."

Philip Knoll

See the upcoming alarm on the watch face. On the watch face showing, tightly press the display, and then tap Customize. Swipe left until you can choose individual facial features, tap the one you'd like to apply for alarms, and then turn the Digital Crown to select the alarm. When you're finished, press the Digital Crown. You can add alarms to these faces:

Chronograph, Color, Mickey Mouse, Modular, Simple, and Utility.

If you like a snooze. Whenever an alarm sounds, you can tap Snooze to wait some minutes before the alarm sounds again. If you do not feel like to allow snooze, tap the alarm in the list of alarms, then turn off Snooze.

To delete an alarm

Open Alarm Clock, tap the alarm in the list, scroll down to the bottom, and then tap Delete.

How to use a timer

The Timer app on Apple smart Watch can assist you to keep track of time. Set timers up to 24 hours.

"Set timer for twenty minutes."

Set a timer. Open Timer, tap hours or minutes, turn t he Digital Crown to adjust, and then tap Start.

If you want to set a timer for longer than 12 hours. A lthough adjusting the timer, tightly press the display, and then tap 24. So that to increase timer length.

How to Add a timer to watch face

If you want to use a timer frequently, add a timer to y our watch face. With the watch face showing,   tightly press the display, and then tap Customize. Swipe left until you can select the individual face appearance, tap the one you'd like to utilize

For the timer, then turn the Digital Crown to select th

e timer. When you're done, press the Digital Crown. You can add a timer to these faces: Chronograph, Color, Mickey Mouse, Modular, Simple, and Utility.

How to set time events with a stopwatch

To time events with much accuracy and simplicity. The Apple smart watch can time full events up to 10 hours, 50 minutes and maintain track of lap or split t imes, then show the results as a list, a graph,or live on your watch face.

The Chronograph of your watch face has the stopwatch built in, and you can add a stopwatch to these faces: Color, Mickey Mouse, Modular, Simple, and Utility.

Switch to the stopwatch

Open the Stopwatch app, or tap the stopwatch on your watch face if you've added it or you're using the Chronograph watch face.

Start, stop, and reset set up.

Tap the Start button. Tap the Lap button to record a lap or split. Tap the Stop button to record the final time. Timing continues, whereas you switch

back to the watch face or open other apps. When you end, tap the Reset button or the Lap button to reset.

How to select the stopwatch format

You can modify the format of the timing display before , after, or during timing. Press the display tightly, desp ite the fact that the stopwatch is showing, and then tap

Analog, Digital, Graph, or Hybrid etc.Switch in-between analog, one-dial and three-dial with splits.

To swipe up on the one dial analog stopwatch appeared to see a separate minute, second, and fourth dials above a scrolling list of lap times.

How to review the results

Review results on the display you used for timing, or modify displays to evaluate your lap times and faster or slowest laps marked with green and red in the format you choose. If the display has a list of lap times, turn the Digital Crown to scroll.

Monitor timing from your watch face.

To keep an eye on a timing session while displaying yo ur usual watch face, add a stopwatch to the face. Your current onwards time will be oberved on the face, and you can tap it to switch to the Stopwatch app and verify your lap times.

How to stop using the stopwatch

If you're using your Stopwatch app, just press the Digi tal Crown. If you're using the Chronograph watch face, the stopwatch controls are constantly on the face- tap the Lap button to reset it.

Philip Knoll

Chapter 9

How to read and reply to messages

I

Scroll down and tap
Reply to respond.

if you want to read incoming text messages on your Apple smart Watch. You can as well reply from Apple Watch, by dictating or selecting a ready response or switch to iPhone to type a new response.

To read a message. You'll think a notification tap or hear an alert sound when a message comes, just raise Apple smart Watch to read it. Turn the Digital Crown to scroll on the Watch. Then open a discussion in the Messages app. Tap the Messages symbol in the notification.

See a photo in your message

Tap the photo to view it, double-tap it to fill up the screen, and drag it to a pan. Whilst you're finished, swipe left from edging of the photo screen to return to the chat. If you like to save the photo, open the message in the Messages app for iPhone, and save it.

Listen to an audio clip in your message

Tap the clip you want to listen. The clip is always deleted after two minutes to save space. If you like to k eep it, tap Keep below the clip. The audio will stay for thirty days, and you can set it to remain longer than th at on the iPhone: go to Settings > Messages, scroll to Audio Messages, tap Expire, then tap a value you want.

View a video with a message

In the Messages app in your Watch, tap a video in a message to begin playing the video full-screen. Tap once to display the playback controls.

Double tap to zoom out and turn the Digital Crown t o regulatthe volume. Then Swipe or alternatively tap t he back button to return to your conversation.

Skip to the top of a long message. In Messages, tap the top of the display.

How to reply to a message. If the message just came, tap its notification, turn the Digital Crown to scroll do wn to the bottom of the message, and then tap Reply. I f it arrived a few seconds ago, swipe down on the watch face to see the message notification, tap it, then scrolls down to the bottom and tap the Reply button.

If you want to mark the message, you already read, ta p Dismiss, or swipe the message. Press the Digital Cro wn of your Watch to dismiss the notification with no marking of the message as read.

To decide how to be notified

When open the Apple smart Watch app on iPhone, t ap My Watch, then tap Messages. Tap Custom to set options for how you like it to notify when you receive any message.

How to send and manage messages

If you want to send a new message. Open the Messages , tightly press the list of chats, and then tap the New

Apple Watch series 4

Message symbol. Tap a contact in the list of recent chat that displays, tap + in the lower left to select from your full list of contacts, or tap the Microphone button to search for somebody in your contacts or to read out a phone number.

There are many ways to write your message:

1. *Use preset replies*

2. *Dictate new text*

3. *Record an audio clip*

4. *Send an animated image*

5. *If you have your iPhone on you can send a map with your location*

6. *You may switch to the iPhone and utilize the full keyboard to type a message*

How to send a preset reply

If you want to reply to a message, you see a list of handy phrases that you can use, just tap the one you w ish to send it. The phrases include related responses based on the last message received and 6 default phrases that you can modify. To reserve your own phrases, open the Apple smart Watch app on iPhone, tap My Watch, go to Messages> Default Replies, then tap a default reply to modify it.

If the predetermined replies are not in the language you like to use, you can modify them by switching the key board for that particular language in the same chat in Messages on iPhone.

If you want to cancel your original reply on Apple sma rt Watch, then replay over again to see the replies in the new language. If you don't like to modify keyboards, you can dictate and send an audio clip in the language of your preference.

To dictate text. Despite the fact that of creating a mess age or reply, tap the Microphone button, say what you want to say, then tap Done. (Please don't forget that you can speak punctuation mark, as well or instance, "did it arrive question mark"). You can also select to send the message as a text message or an audio clip, now tap your choice. If you select an audio clip, the rece iver gets a voice message to listen to, but not a text message read.

If you are using more than one language and your dictation isn't transcribed in the right language for a ch at, you can still send it as an audio clip. To modify the dictation language, change the Siri language on your iPhone in Settings > General > Siri, and then start a new chat.

If you want to send dictated text as an audio clip

If you want to send all your dictated text as an audio clip, you don't require selecting it each time. Open the Apple smart Watch app on your iPhone, tap My Watch, go to Messages > Audio Messages, and then tap an option.

Philip Knoll

Include an animated image

Whilst creating a message or respond, tap the image button, and then swipe to look through the available images. Turn the Digital Crown to scroll down and adjust the image, for instance, turns the smile into a frown gesture. On faces, drag left or right across the eyes or mouth to modify the expression more. To see other image types, swipe to the next pages. The last page lists traditional emoji. When you find the right icon, tap it to add it to your message, and then tap send.

To share your location

If you want to send a map showing your current locatio ns to your friend, tightly press the display while viewing the chart, and then taps Send my Location.

You should ensure that your paired iPhone, Share My Location is turned on in Settings > iCloud > Share My Location.

Do you want to see if your messages were sent? Swipe left on the conversation in the Messages conversation list.

Philip Knoll

How to view messages detail information

Tightly press the display while viewing the conversation, then taps Details it will show the contact information of the other participant(s) in the conversation. Alternatively, swipes left on the conversation, and then tap Details.

How to delete a conversation

Swipe left on the conversation, tap Trash, and then tap the Trash to confirm.

Chapter 10

Digital Touch of your Apple Watch

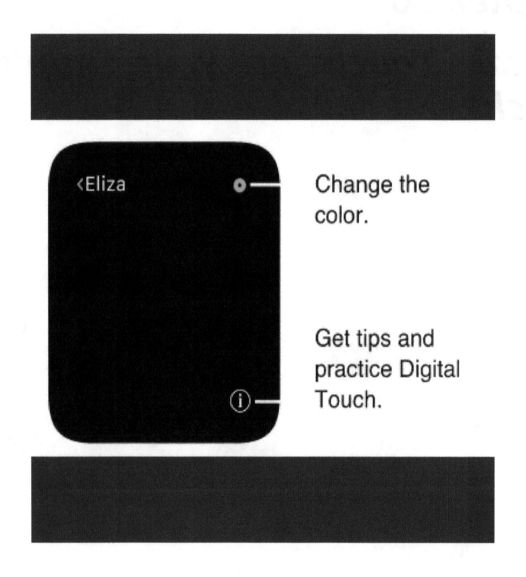

‹Eliza

Change the color.

Get tips and practice Digital Touch.

Apple Watch series 4

The *main function of Digital Touch is that you can send sketches, taps,* or *your heartbeat to your friend with an Apple smart Watch.*

To open a Digital Touch

Press the side button of your Apple Watch to see your friends, then tap a friend and tap the Digital To uch button below his photo. You only see the Digital Touch symbol if your friend has an Apple smart Watch.

Philip Knoll

How to send a Digital Touch

To send any of a sketch, a pattern of taps, or even your heartbeat. In the screenshot that follows, the image on the left shows what is sent, and the image on the right shows the notification that has been receive d.

To experience a Digital Touch someone has sent, just tap on a notification. Send a sketch. Draw on the screen

Send a tap

Tap the screen to send a single tap or tap repeatedly to send a tap pattern.

Replay the tap pattern

Share your heartbeat. Place two fingers on the display until you feel your heartbeat and see it animated on the screen.

The Mail

The E-mail on your Apple Watch

How to read mail

On your Apple smart Watch, open the Mail app, turn the Digital Crown to scroll down the message list, and then tap a message. To read the message or reply on your iPhone, just swipe up on the Mail symbol in the lower-left corner of the iPhone Lock screen.

Read mail in a notification.

If you want to set Apple smart Watch to show email notifications, you can read a new message right in the notification. Tap the notification when it first displays or swipe down on the watch face to see notifications you 've received, then taps an email notification.

To dismiss the notification, swipe down from the top or tap Dismiss at the end of the message.

Apple Watch series 4

If you don't receive notifications for an email, go to Set tings > Notifications' on your iPhone and verify to see if you have notifications turned on for e-mail.

Your Apple watch configures most text styles and som e formats; quoted text displays in a different color relat ively than as an indentation. If you receive an HTML message with compound elements, Apple smart Watch tries to display a text alternative of the message. It is better to try reading the message on your iPhone in its place. Switch to iPhone.

Philip Knoll

Some messages are simpler to read in full on iPhone, w ake your iPhone, then swipe up on the email symbol in the lower left corner of the lock screen.

Then go back to the top of a long email message. Turn the Digital Crown to scroll down swiftly, or just tap the top of the display.

How to open Phone or Maps

Tap a phone number in a mail message to open Phone , or an address to open Maps. Observe the complete ad dress or subject line. Tap in the in the field or the subje ct line. Apple watch opens the mail message in its own window; as a result, you can see all the details.

182

To reply to email. You require using iPhone to create a reply-just wake
your iPhone and swipe up on the mail symbol in the lo wer-left corner of the Lock screen.

How to manage your email

Flag a mail message. When you're reading the message in Mail on Apple smart Watch, tightly press the display, and then tap Flag. If you're looking at the message list, swipe left on the message, then tap More. You can fag the message if you preview it in a notification. You should swipe to the Flag button at the bottom of the message. You can also unplug a message that has previously been flagged.

Whenever you swipe left on a message thread, the action you select are such Flag, Mark as Unread, or Delete applies to the thread.

To modify the style flag. Open the Apple smart Watc h app on your iPhone, tap My Watch, and then go to Mail > Custom > Flag Style.

Mark an email as read or unread.

When you're reading a message in Mail on Apple sm art Watch, tightly press the display, and then taps Un read or Read. If you're looking at the message list, swipe left on the message, and then taps More.

To delete your email

If you're reading the message in Mail on Apple smart Watch, tightly press the display, and then tap Trash. If you're looking at the message list, swipe left on the message, and then tap Trash.

You can alternatively delete a message from its notification. Scroll down to the bottom of the message, and then tap Trash.

185

However, if your account is placed to archive messages, you'll see an Archive button as an alternative of a Trash button.

How to select which mailbox appears on Apple smart Watch. Open your Apple Watch app on iPhone, tap My Watch, then go to Mail > Include Mail. You can indicate only one mailbox, although if you don't select a mailbox, you can see all the content from all inboxes.

To customize alerts

To adapt your alert open the Apple smart Watch app on iPhone, tap My Watch, then turn on Mail >

Show Alerts. Tap every account or group, turn on the option to be alerted, and then select Sound or Haptic.

If your message list is long

To build your mail list more condensed, you may reduce the number of lines of preview text shown for every email in the list. Open the Apple smart Watch app on iPhone, tap My Watch, go to Mail > Message
Preview, then select to show two lines of the message, o ne line, or none at all.

Chapter 11
Phone Calls on Apple Watch

How to answer phone calls

It is a very significant idea about avoiding any distract ions that might lead to dangerous situations.

Answer a call.

When you see the incoming call notification, raise your wrist to wake Apple Mart Watch and identify who's calling. Tap the Answer butto on Apple Watch to cha t using the microphone and speaker on Apple Watch. To scroll down to answer the call using an iPhone or send a text message in its place, turn the Digital Crow n to scroll down, and then select an option.

Hold a call.

Tap on "Answer on iPhone" to put the call on hold until you can continue it on your paired iPhone. The c aller hears a continual sound unless you pick up the call. If you can't find your iPhone in range, tap the ping iPhone button on Apple Watch to locate it.

Switch a call from Apple Watch to your iPhone

Whilst chatting on Apple smart Watch, just swipe up on the Phone symbol in the bottom-left corner of the iPhone Lock screen. Alternatively, if your iPhone is unlocked, tap the green bar at the top of the screen.

Change the call volume.

To adjust the speaker volume when chatting on Apple Watch, turn the Digital Crown while on the call or t ap the volume symbols on the screen. Tap the Mute but ton to mute your end of the call for an instant if you're on a conference call.

You can swiftly mute an incoming call by pressing the palm of your hand on the watch display and holding it there for 3 seconds. You must initially turn on the opt ion in the Apple smart Watch app on iPhone. Go to My Watch > Sounds and Haptics and turn on Cover to Mute.

To send a call to voicemail

Tap on the red Decline button in the incoming call notification.

If you want to listen to voicemail. If a caller leaves a voicemail, you get a notification. Tap the Play button in the notification to listen. Nevertheless, if you like to listen to voicemail later, then open the Phone app, and tap Voicemail.

How to make phone calls

"Call Max."

If the one you're calling is one of your favorites, press the side button, turn the Digital Crown, or tap their initial name, then tap the call button. If they're not in your contacts list, open the Phone app, and then tap favorites or contacts. Turn the Digital Crown to scroll down, and tap the name you want to call.

The call information on Apple watch

When you're talking about the iPhone, you can view call information on your Apple Watch in the Phone app. You can as well end the call from Apple Watch, especially, if you're using earphones or a headset.

Chapter 12

Apple Watch Calendars and Reminders

How to verify and update your calendar

The Calendar app on Apple smart Watch shows ever y event you've scheduled or been invited from today to the next week. Apple smart Watch displays events for all calendars you have used on your iPhone.

View a monthly calendar

If you like to view your calendar

Open Calendar from the Watch Home screen or swipe up on the watch face, swipe to the Calendar glance, then tap. You can tap today's date on your watch face if you've already added the calendar to the face.

"What's your next event?"

Review today's events.

Just open the Calendar, and then turn the Digital Crown to scroll. Swipe right on today's timeline or jump to the current time. To see event details, such as time, location, invite status, and notes, tap the event.

But if you like to switch among the daily timeline and a single list of your events. Tightly press the display wh ile you're viewing a daily calendar, and then tap List or Day.

View a different day.

In Day view, just swipe left on today's calendar to see the next day.

Swipe right to go back

You may not be able to see any day before today, or more than 7 days total. To jump back to the current day and time, tightly press the display, and then tap Today. In List view, then turn the Digital Crown.

To view a full month calendar. Tap < in the upper left of any daily calendar. Tap the monthly calendar to return to Day view.

Philip Knoll

Add and change your event.

Switch to the Calendar app on your iPhone, then add the event there. If you're viewing at your calendar on Apple smart Watch, just wake iPhone and swipe up on the Calendar symbol in the lower-left corner of the Lock screen to open the Calendar.

"Build calendar event titled Gym for May 20 4 PM."

To display the date or an upcoming event on your watc h face. You can add some mixture of day and date to several of the watch faces: for an instant, Modular, Color, Utility, Simple, or Chronograph. The Modular , Chronograph, and Mickey Mouse faces can display the next upcoming event. Tightly press the display whil e looking the watch face, swipe to a face, and then tap Customize.

Respond to an invitation

If you see the invitation when it comes, just swipe or turn the Digital Crown to scroll to the bottom of the n otification, then tap Accept, Maybe, or Decline. If you find out the notification later, tap it in your list of notifications, then scroll and respond. If you're alrea dy in the Calendar app, now tap the event to respond.

Contact an event organizer.

If you like to email the event organizer, tightly press this display while you're viewing at the event details. To send a voice message or call, just tap on the organizer's name in the event details.

Time to leave

You can to-do list a "leave now" alert based on the anticipated travel time to an event you create. Open the Calendar app on your iPhone, tap the event, tap

Edit, tap Travel Time, and turn it on. You'll obtain an alert that takes travel time into account.

The settings change.

Open the Apple smart Watch app on your iPhone, tap My Watch, and then tap Calendar.

How to set and respond to reminders

When there is no reminder app on Apple smart Watch, but Apple Watch notifies you of reminders you make in the Reminders app on your iPhone. And on any other or Mac, that's signed in using your Apple

ID. You can make reminders using Siri on Apple smart Watch.

Respond to a reminder.

If you see the reminder notification when it comes, just swipe to the bottom of the reminder, and then tap Snooze, Completed, or Dismiss. If you find out the no tification afterward, tap it in your list of notifications, then scroll down and respond.

Set a reminder.

To utilize Siri on Apple Watch

Press and hold the Digital Crown, then speak. Altern atively, just raise your wrist and say "Hi Siri, set a re minder." You can set reminders on your iPhone or other device such as IOS device or Mac that is signed in using your Apple ID.

Chapter 13

Your health and fitness

How to track your daily activity

The Activity app on your Apple Watch keeps a trail of your association all over the day and helps sup pose you to meet your fitness set goals. The app can als o track how frequently you stand up, how greatly you move, and how many minutes of exercise you perform, and it provides an easy graphic ring of your daily activity.

Apple Watch series 4

The main goal is to sit less, move more, and get some e xercise by finishing each ring every day. The Activity a pp on your iPhone keeps a long-term record of all your daily and weekly activity.

However, you should take note that Apple Watch can detect the heart rate using its sensor, and the Apple sm art Watch apps are not medical devices and intended solely for fitness purposes only.

Philip Knoll

Getting started

For the first time, you open Activity on your Apple smart Watch, swipe left to read the Move, Exercise, and Stand descriptions, then tap Get Started. Enter t he essential information by tapping Sex, Age, Weight, and Height, and then turn the Digital Crown to set and tap Continue. Lastly, tap Start Moving.

You should also enter your birthdates, sex, height, and weight in the Apple smart Watch app on iPhone. In the Apple Watch app, tap My Watch, and then tap Health.

Verify your progress.

Swipe up on your watch face, then swipe to the Activit y glances at every time to see how you're doing. Tap the glance to open the Activity app and swipe to see the pe rsonal activities. The Move ring indicates how many ac tive calories you've burned. The exercise ring shows ho w many minutes of brisk activity you've done. The Sta nd ring shows how many times in the day you've stood for at least 1 minute per hour. Swipe upon an activity or turn the Digital Crown to see your progress as a form of a graph.

An overlapping ring means you've exceeded your goal. Watch for achievement awards, if you have that feature turned on.

Check your activity history

To open the Activity app on your iPhone, tap on a date in the calendar to see a breakdown for that day. You 'll see how many steps you took and the particular distance you covered, in addition to Move, exercise, and Stand info.

Regulate your goals.

Open Activity on Apple smart Watch and tightly press the display until you see the prompt to modify your Move goal.

On Monday every week, you'll also be notified about t he previous week's achievements, and you can regulate your daily Move goal for the coming week. Apple Wat ch suggests goals based on your prior performance.

Control activity notifications.

Reminders can help you when it comes to meeting goals. Apple smart Watch can let you know if you're on the trail or falling behind your activity goals. It can even alert you if you've been sitting for too long.

Philip Knoll

To select which reminders and alerts you'd like to see, open the Apple smart Watch app on your iPhone, tap My Watch, then tap Activity.

Monitor your workouts

The Workout app on your Apple Watch gives you the tools to control your personal workout sessions. It lets you set explicit goals, likes time, distance, or calories, then trails your progress, nudges you along the way, and précised your results. You can also use the Activity app on your iPhone to analysis your entire workout history.

Start a workout.

Apple Watch series 4

Open Workout, and then tap the workout kind you're going for. As you use the app and select workouts, the order of workouts will reflect your preferences.

On your goal screen, swipe left and right to select a calorie, time, or distance goal (or no goal), then turn the Digital Crown or tap + / - to set.

When you're prepared to go, tap Start. If you're measuring caloric or time, you can leave your iPhone at the back and exercise with just Apple smart Watch. However, for the most perfect distance measurements outdoors, it better to take iPhone a long.

The Outdoors and Indoor Walk, Run, Cycle is differe d workouts because the Apple smart Watch calculates the calorie burn another way for each. For example th e indoor workouts, Apple Watch relies mostly on your heart rate readings for calorie estimates, but for outdo or workouts, Apple smart Watch works in combinati on with your iPhone that has GPS to calculate speed and distance. Those standards, values, along with your heart rate, it is used to estimate the number of calories burned.

Checking your progress

To check the completion ring throughout your workout for a swift sign of your progress. Swipe on the lower h alf of the screen to review elapsed time, average pace, distance covered, calories used, and heart rate. As an a lternative to viewing the progress rings, you can select to see your distance, calorie, or time values numerically. Open the Apple smart Watch app on iPhone, tap My Watch, then turn on Workout > Show Goal Metric.

Pause and resume.

If you want to stop the workout at any given time, tightly press the display, and then tap Pause. In the w ay to carry on, tightly press the display again, then tap Resume.

Conserve power at long workout

You can save power by disabling the heart rate sensor during long walking and running workouts. Your calorie burn estimate might not be as correct. Open the Apple smart Watch app on iPhone, tap My Watch, and then turn on Workout > Power Saving Mode.

End the workout.

Whenever you reach your stated goal, you'll hear an al arm. If you're feeling fine and want to continue, go ahe ad. Apple smart Watch continues to collect data until you notify it to stop.

When you're ready, tightly press the display, and then tap end. Turn the Digital Crown to scroll through the results summary, then tap Save or Discard at the bottom.

Review your workout account.

Just open the Activity app on your iPhone, then tap a date. Scroll down to see your workouts listed there the Move, Stand and Exercise summaries. Swipe left on a workout to see more details of it.

Philip Knoll

How to check your heart rate

If you want to get the best results, the back of Apple smart watch needs skin contact for the appearance like wrist detection, haptic notifications, and the heart rate sensor. When wearing an Apple smart Watch with the right fit. You must not wear it too tight, but also n ot too loose, and with room for your skin to breathe; th is will keep you comfortable and allow the sensors to d o their function. You may yearn for tightening Apple smart Watch for workouts, and then loosen the band when you're done. Furthermore, the sensors will solely work only when you wear Apple smart Watch on the top of your wrist.

View your present heart rate.

Swipe up on the watch face, then swipe to the Heartbe at glance to determine your heart rate and see your last reading. Just tap the heart in the glance to take a new reading.

Heart rate checking during a workout

Just, Swipe on the lower half of the workout progress screen.

Philip Knoll

How to keep your Apple Watch data accurate

Apple Watch always uses the bio data information you give about your height, weight, gender, and age so t hat, to compute how many calories you burn, how dist ance you travel, and other data. In addition, the more you run with the workout app you have, the more Ap ple smart watch learns your fitness rank.
Moreover, the more precisely it can calculate approxim ately the calories you've burned during aerobic activity.

Apple Watch series 4

Your iPhone GPS, permit Apple smart Watch to ach ieve even more far accuracy. For instance, if you carry an iPhone while using the Workout app on a run, Apple smart Watch uses the iPhone GPS to calibrate your stride out. Then later, if you're not carrying the iPhone, or if you're working out where a GPS networ k is not available (for instance, if you are indoors), A pple smart watch uses the already stored information about your stride to measure distance.

Philip Knoll

Update on your height and weight.

Just open the Apple smart Watch app on iPhone, tap My Watch, tap Health, Weight, or Height, and change.

Chapter 14

Apple Watch Pay and Passbook

How to make a purchase with Apple Pay

If you want to purchase things online, you can use A pple Pay on Aple smart Watch to make purchases i n stores that acknowledge contactss payments. Set up an Apple Pay in the Apple smart Watch app on your iPhone, and now you can make purchases, even if you don't have an iPhone.

If you unpaired Apple Watch, disable your passcode, or turn of wrist detection because you can't use Apple Pay.

You can add up to 8 credit or debit cards; they'll appear at the top of the stack in your Passbook app, a bove your passes. The last 4 or 5 digits of your credit or debit card number shown on the front of a payment card.

Get set up on Apple Pay on your Apple Watch.

Despite the fact that, you've already set up an Apple Pay on your iPhone using the Passbook app, you   also need to add the credit or debit cards to use on Apple smart Watch. Have your credit or debit card handy, and then open the Apple smart Watch app on your iPhone. Tap My Watch, tap Passbook and App le Pay, tap Add Credit or Debit Card, and then tap Next. If you get a supported credit or debit card on file with iTunes or the App Store, enter the card's secu rity code first. Or else, use the iPhone camera to snap t he information on your credit or debit card, and then c ompete in any information required, with the card secu rity code. You must know that your card issuer someti mes requires other detail steps to prove your identity. If so, select a verification option, *tap Verify, and then tap Enter Code to complete your verification.*

Add another credit or debit card.

In your Apple watch app on iPhone, tap My Watch, tap Passbook & Apple Pay, tap Add Credit or Debit Card, then follow the on-screen commands.

Select your default card.

In your Apple watch app on your iPhone, tap My W atch, tap Passbook & Apple Pay, tap Default Card, and then choose the desired card.

How to make pay for a purchase

If you want to pay for a purchase. Just double click the side button, swipe to modify cards, and then hold Apple smart Watch within a few centimeters of the contactless card reader, with the display facing the reader. A gentle pulse and tone authenticate the payment information was sent.

Find the device account number for a card.

Whenever you make a payment with Apple Watch, th e Device Account Number of the card is sent with the payment to the merchant party. To find the last 4 or 5 digits of this number, just open the Apple smart Wat ch app on iPhone, tap My Watch, tap Passbook & Apple Pay, then tap a card.

Remove a card from Apple Pay

Just open Passbook on Apple Watch, tap to choose a card, tightly press the card, and then tap delete. Altern atively, open the Apple smart Watch app on your iPh one, tap My Watch, tap Passbook & Apple Pay, tap the card, then tap Remove.

If the Apple smart watch is stolen or lost

Whenever your Apple Watch is lost or stolen, sign in t o your account at iCloud.com and remove your cards. Go to Settings > My Devices, select the device, and click Remove All. You can also call the company of your cards.

How to use Passbook

Your Passbook app on Apple Watch can keep your b oarding passes, movie tickets, loyalty cards, and much more in one place. Your passes in Passbook on your iPhone automatically sync to Apple Watch when you've turned on Mirror iPhone in the Watch app. Firstly scans a pass on Apple smart Watch to verify in for a fight, get into a movie, or redeem a coupon. To set options for your passes on Apple smart Watch, just open the Apple Watch app on your iPhone, tap My Watch, then tap Passbook & Apple Pay.

Ways to use a pass.

If a notification for a pass shows on Apple smart Watch, tap the notification to display the pass. You m ay have to scroll down to get to the barcode. Alternativ ely, open Passbook, choose the pass, and then present the barcode on the pass to the scanner.

The way to rearrange passes.

On your iPhone, open the Passbook app, and drag to rearrange passes. The order will reflect on Apple smart watch.

When done with a pass? To delete the pass on your iP hone. Just open the Passbook app, tap the pass, tap, and then tap Delete.

Chapter 15

Apple Watch Maps and Directions

How to explore the map

Your Apple smart Watch has a Maps glance for a swift look at your surrounding location, and a full Maps app for exploring and getting directions.

Apple Watch series 4

"Show town on the map."

View a map.

Just open the Maps app on Apple smart watch. Or, for a fast look at your location, swipe up on your watch face, then swipe to the Maps glance. Tap the Maps glance to open the full Maps app.

Pan and zoom.

If you want to pan the map, drag with one finger. But if you want to zoom in or out, turn the Digital Crown. You can double-tap the map to zoom in on the spot you tap. Tap the tracking button in the lower left to get back to your recent location.

Searching the map

As you are viewing the map, tightly press the display, tap Search, and then tap Dictate or tap a location in the list of places you've explored recently.

Getting a data about the landmark or location

Just tap the location on the map, then turn the Digital Crown to scroll the information. Tap < in the upper left to return to the map.

To stick a pin

Just touch and hold the map where you want the pin to go, wait for the pin to drop, and then let go. At the moment, you can tap the pin for address information, or utilize it as the starting point or destination for directions. To move the pin, just drop a new one in the new location.

How to find the accurate address on the map. Here just drop a pin on the location, then tap the pin to see address information.

Philip Knoll

To call a location

Just tap the phone number in the location information. To switch to iPhone, swipe up on the Phone symbol in the lower-left corner of the Lock screen, then tap the green bar at the top of the screen.

How to see your contact's address on the map

As you are viewing the map, tightly press the display, tap Contacts, turn the Digital Crown to scroll, and then tap the contact.

Get your location.

Just open Maps, then tap the recent location arrow in the lower left. Or swipe to the Maps glance, which always indicates where you are. If you have a future calendar event, the Maps glance shows directions to it.

How to get your directions

If you want to get your directions to any landmark or map pin. Just open Maps, then tap the target landmark or map pin. Scroll down the location detail until you see Directions, then tap Walking or Driving. Whenever you're all set to go, tap Start, then follow the directions.

To get directions to a search result or contact. As you are viewing the map, tightly press the display, and then tap Search or Contacts.

To ask Siri for directions

Just say to Siri where you'd like to go.

How to follow the directions

Subsequent to your tap to start and head off on your first leg, Apple smart Watch uses tapping to allow you know when to turn. A stable series of 12 taps means turn right at the intersection you're approaching ; three pairs of two taps means turn left. But if not sure what your target location looks like? You'll feel a vibration when you're on the last leg, and again when you arrive.

Check your progress.

Just swipe left on the current step of your directions, or tap the dots at the bottom of the screen to see a map view.

How to estimated time, Just of arrival, tightly press to stop directions.

To find out when you'll get there.

Philip Knoll

Just look in the upper-left corner for your estimated time of arrival. The Current time is in the upper right.

The end directions to you get there

Tightly press the display, and then tap Stop Directions

.

Chapter 16

Play music on your iPhone

You can use the Music app or the Now Playing glance on Apple Watch to control music playback on your iPhone.

"Play Panda Bear."

Philip Knoll

Play music on the iPhone.

Just open Music to Apple smart Watch. Surf through playlists, albums, artists, or songs until you see a list of songs you like, and then tap a song to play it.

However, if you don't spot the music you're expecting, make sure iPhone, not Apple Watch, is your source. Tightly press the display, tap Source, then Return to track list.

Tap to see the album art. Firmly press for playback options. Skip to previous or next track. Tap -/+ or turn Digital Crown to adjust volume.

See album art for the existing song. Tap the album name above the playback controls. Tap again to return to the controls.

To send an audio to another device with AirPlay. As you are viewing the playback controls, tightly press the display, tap AirPlay, then select a destination.

To shuffle or repeat songs

As you are viewing the playback controls, tightly press the display, and then tap Shuffle or Repeat.

Controlling playback with the glance

Just use the Now Playing glance for swift control. Swipe up on the watch face, then swipe to the playback controls. But if you don't see the Now Playing glance, open the Apple Watch app on your iPhone, tap My Watch, then turn on Music > Show in Glances.

How to play music on Apple watch

You can store your music on Apple smart Watch, and then listen to it via Bluetooth headphones or speakers without your iPhone close by.

Store a song on Apple Watch.

Apple Watch series 4

Just open the Apple Watch app on your iPhone, tap My Watch, go to Music>Synced Playlist, then select the playlist of songs you like to move to Apple smart Watch.

Then, put the Apple smart watch on its charger to entire the sync.

While the music has been synced, open the Settings ap p on Apple Watch, go to General > about, and look below Songs to see the number of songs copied.

You can also use the Music app on iPhone to make a playlist specifically for music you want to listen to on Apple smart Watch.

Philip Knoll

How to pair Bluetooth headphones or speakers

You should follow the instruction guide that came with the headphones or speakers to set them in discover y mode.

When the Bluetooth device is ready, open the Settings app on Apple smart Watch, tap Bluetooth, then tap the device when it displays.

To play songs stored on Apple smart Watch.

Just open Music on Apple Watch, tightly press the display, tap Source, then select Watch.

To control playback

Swipe to the Now Playing glance for swift control. Swipe up on the watch face, then swipe to the playback controls. You can control playback using the Music app.

How to limit the songs stored on Apple W atch.

Just open the Apple Watch app on your iPhone, tap My Watch, go to Music> Playlist Limit, then select a storage limit or the maximum number of songs to be stored on Apple smart Watch.

See how music is stored on Apple smart watch.

Just on Apple smart Watch, open the Settings app, go to General > about, and look under Songs.

Chapter 17

Using an Apple smart Watch as Remote Control

How to control music on a Mac or PC

You can use the Remote app on Apple smart watch t o play music in iTunes on your computer on the same Wi-Fi network.

Add an iTunes library.Just open the remote app on Apple smart Watch, then tap Add Device +. In

247

Philip Knoll

iTunes on your computer,
click the Remote button close to the top of the iTunes
window, then enter the 4-digit code displayed on Apple
smart Watch.

Don't stare for the Remote button in iTunes before yo
u tap Add Device on Apple Watch-the button   shows
only when a remote is trying to connect. In iTunes 12
and later, the Remote button is in the upper left, under
the Volume slider. But in iTunes 11 and earlier, the
Remote button is in the upper right, below the Search
field.

Apple Watch series 4

Select a library to play from. If you have one library, you should be good to go. However, if you're adding m ore than one library, tap the one you like when you ope n Remote on Apple smart Watch.

If you're already playing music, tap the Back button in the upper left of the playback controls, and then tap the library.

To control playback. Just use the playback controls in the Remote app.

Philip Knoll

The way to remove a library

In your Remote app on Apple watch, tap the Back button in the upper left to view your devices, tightly press the display, and then tap edit. When the device symbol jiggle, tap x on the one you like to remove, then tap Remove. If that was your only remote device, you're finished. Or else, tap the checkmark to finish editing.

How to control Apple TV with Apple Smart Watch

You can also use Apple smart Watch as a remote control for your Apple TV when you're connected to the same Wi-Fi network.

Pairing Apple smart Watch with Apple TV

If your iPhone has never joined the Wi-Fi network that Apple TV is on, just join it now. Then, open the Remote app on Apple Watch and tap Add Device +. On your Apple TV, go to Settings > General > Re motes, select your Apple watch, and then enter the pas scode displayed on Apple smart Watch.

When the pairing successfully an icon appears next to Apple Smart Watch, it's ready to control your Apple TV.

How to control Apple TV

You must make sure that your Apple TV is awake. Open the Remote app on Apple smart Watch, select Apple TV, then swipe up, down, left, or right to move through Apple TV menu options.

Tap to select the selected item. Tap the Menu button to go back, or

touch and hold it to return to the top menu. Tap the P lay/Pause button to pause or resume playback. Tap to go back or touch and hold to return to main menu.

Control another device.

Swipe to move through Apple TV menu options;

Tap to select.

Play or pause selection.

To Unpaired and remove Apple TV.

Philip Knoll

Just on your Apple TV, go to Settings > General> Remotes, then choose your Apple smart Watch under i OS Remotes to remove it. Then, open the Remote ap on Apple smart Watch and, when the "lost link" mes sage appears, tap Remove.

Chapter 18

Things you did not know about Apple Watch.

The Apple Watch has been released recently it comes with many things you didn't know. Therefore, we are going to tell you about tips that you didn't kno w about Apple Watch series 4. The recent design of A pple Watch was obviously better than the previous mo dels. Firstly, what to do when you get a new Apple W atch. The first thing you want to do is the ability to m ake use of a great new inforgraph of your Watch, whic h will take you to the entire Apple Watch face. Of cou rse, this is greater than the previous generation of Apple Watch.

Here there are many different functions, from the walk ie talkie, weather and many more. However, you migh t scroll down to anyone you want ranging from a one that more center for you.

From timer, an activity you can also change these arou nd moving your location to where you like in the Watc

h. When that's done the next thing to do is to center areas of your Watch. You may choose a different setting such as the digital crown, time, the eart h and even measuring your heart rate as well as setting the inner configurations such as time.

Here you may even choose a different clock face pattern and different like wake-up application.

In the inforgraph, you can set different clock faces. This new inforgraph is unique concerning Apple Watc h series.

Philip Knoll

The next thing to do is set the inforgraph-up you want to mark it. With this, you can open your Mac book but only when you log in into your Watch. We want t o do the basic setting, go to security and allow your Ap ple Watch to make your Mac that is simple and can be easily paired with your Mac, Mac-pro or any types of Mac do have to just use your Apple Watch.

The next thing you may want to do is to set Activity shearing. Open up the activity on your phone, then go to the sharing button, you can see that you can invite your friends. From your Watch App on your phone, you can increase the brightness of your Watch. In addition, you can also change the textures, to increase the size of the text where it is a little bit easier to read messages, but you may make it a little bit smaller.

The next features you are going to set-up when you get new Apple Watch is the most serious features, I hope you will not use it, but it is better to set up because it is very important to have it in your Apple Watch. So its emergency response system of your Watch. From your phone, open Apple Watch app for phone, it allows you to call the emergency number which you are going to include the number into the app. Therefore, if you set it up it could reach that number in case of an e mergency that number could get a notification that you need help.

Another thing that is very important is setting up a fall detection. This app will ask whether Watch has fallen or not within your hand reach, it will automatically ask you, so that you have the ability to make sure you Watch is safe.

Another important setup is to set —up your heart rate so that if you are in a workout it will appear active, you can set the haptic feature so that to send the information to your emergency contact when needed.

Apple Watch series 4

Another good app is using the eBay app that you should download on your phone open it in safari browser, it is a wonderful app that I'm sure when you download it you will enjoy it. Open the new page and write a bit. lygetbetes bonus

Which you can get 10% back bonus from eBay cash back.

Write your email and download eBay app. That app contains 10% cash guaranty it has VIP 30% and all coupons that available for purchase and you can also download it on your computer, when you check any marketplace, online you will see the coupon code such as

Walmart, JXV, Dr. ax, and eBay.

You can click on the shop now. But mark you Amaz on does not have that 10% cash back guarantee. You can do all there exactly eBay when clicking the shop now. I highly recommended using this app because I usually use it to buy online and get 10% discount.

Another thing you will do when you get a new Apple Watch series 4.On your phone can explore the whole gallery of your Watch; you may view inforgraph and se lect any Watch face you like. You can also view all ap plications for your Apple Watch and you may get man y applications for your Apple Watch for better performances.

If you want to set and optimize your watch go to the setting on your Watch open setting, you can set it up to 15,30, and 70 minutes here you can set how long you want your Watch to stay in standby.

How to use Apple Watch

The Apple Watch may perhaps not have become as ve ry important as your smart phone. But since Apple first took the veil of secrecy of its smart watch in 2015, the Apple Watch has motionlessly managed to fill a need for many users, and in addition to the cellular connectivity in the latest series makes this gadget even more valuable. The key for making the Apple Watch series 4 an essential part of your life? So it is very important to know how to get the most of it. We have an in-depth guide to Apple's Watch, but let's begin with some quick tips and tricks that put up the Apple Watch even easier to use.

Switching between Apple Apps

If you want to switch between your Apps, to go back t o your most recently used apps, double tap the Digital Crown.

Switching in-between your Watch Face

You might want to set up multiple watch faces for different purposes — one with a minimum face for those times when you don't like a cluttered edge, the other with a more fun display. To switch back and forth, you can just swipe to the left and right from the watch face.

Rearranging your applications in the Dock

Apple Watch could overhaul the Dock, which gives you simple access to your most frequently, used apps.

Philip Knoll

However, what if you want to change the order in which those apps appear how to about it.

Just Open the Watch app on your iPhone and select Dock.

Select whether you want your Dock ordered by recently used apps or favorites. Tap Edit to choose your favorite apps in your Watch. You can add up to 10 apps to your Dock, which is available by pressing the side button on your watch.

Muting an Incoming Call

When a call comes in, in the middle of a meeting, just cover your Apple Watch with your hand to mute it.

How to Take a Screenshot

Whenever, you like to take a screenshot with your Apple Watch, primarily, make sure that the feature is enabled in the Watch app on your iPhone. Then Tap General from the Watch app's main screen, then scroll down and tap Enable Screenshots. When t his feature enabled, to take a screenshot, you should ju st press the Digital Crown and the Side Button at the same time (Alternatively, hold the Digital Crown and then press the Side Button). The Screenshots are stored in the Camera Roll on your iPhone.

To Send a Friend Your Location

It's very easy to let your friends know where you are, u sing the Messages app on your Apple Watch. Open a conversation in the Messages. Vigor Touch the screen and tap Send Location.

Reading and responding to messages

To read a new message in your Watch, raise your wrist after reading a message notification. Nevertheless , to dismiss the message, lower your arm.

Sending a text message

If you want to send a new text, open the Apple Watch 's Messages app. Its icon, sign is identical to the one on your iPhone. Force Touch the screen and then tap New Message.

How to delete email

Some tips on how to get rid of an email directly from your watch area.

Philip Knoll

On your Apple Watch, open the Mail app Swipe left on any email. Alternatively, tap the trash to delete the message.

How to clear Your Notifications

A lot of Notifications piling up? Here is how to dismiss them.

From your watch face, swipe down from the top of the screen to display your notification. Force touches the display, then tap clear all.

How set focus and exposure in the App camera

The camera on your Apple Watch allows you to use the watch as a remote for your iPhone camera. Launch the app, and tap any place on the preview image on your Watch to set the focus and exposure.

Pausing or ending your workout

With a workout in progress, open the Workout app. Swipe right on the display. Tap End or Pause.

Philip Knoll

Deleting Apps from Your Watch

If you want to delete Apps from Watch, Deleting an app from your Apple Watch works the same way it d oes on an iPhone. From the face of your Apple Watch or any app, press the Digital Crown to go to the Watch's home screen.

Tap and hold any app icon. Tap the small X that appears on any third-party app icon to remove the app from your Apple Watch. Then Tap Delete App to confirm.

Changing Audio sources; *The tricks to control the device, your phone, or your watch. From which you* *play music. In the Music app, Force Touch the display, then taps Source.*

Choose iPhone to play music from your phone. Select Apple Watch to play music from your watch on a Bluetooth speaker and headphone.

How to Switch Views in a Calendar

Open the Calendar app, and then select a day, and then Force Touch the display.

Select List to view a list of upcoming events or Up Ne xt to see the cards of upcoming events. Tap Today to skip to the current day in either view.

Philip Knoll

Control Mickey/Minnie Mouse Speak the Time

The Apple Watch has two different faces versions featuring either Mickey or Minnie Mouse. In addition , they can pull off a little trick.

How to switch to the Mickey/Minnie Mouse watch face

Tap the screen and any character that you have selected will announce the current time. (You can also disable this under Sounds & Haptics in either the Apple Watch's Settings app or the Watch app on your iPhone.)

How to Activate Siri

In order to activate Siri, just pull up Siri for voice commands, press and hold the Digital Crown on the Watch. Otherwise, raise your wrist and say "Hey Siri."

How to Find Your Phone

Your phone is constantly a quick tap away when you're wearing an Apple Watch.

On the watch face, swipe up on the display to bring up Control Center. Then tap the Find Phone icon in the right. This will make Your iPhone play a sound.

How to unpaired Your Apple Watch

If you want to upgrade your iPhone, you'll make sure you unpair it with your Apple Watch. Open the

Apple Watch series 4

Apple Watch app on your iPhone, and choose your Apple Watch from the main menu.

On the Apple Watch next screen, tap the "i" button next to your Watch.

Tap Unpair Apple Watch. (Remember this will back up all settings from your Apple smart Watch onto your iPhone and then erase your Apple Watch.)

How to Call Emergency Services

The first Emergency SOS was added into 2016's watch 3 update. However, this can also work on Apple series 4.

Philip Knoll

If you like to call emergency service, Press and hold the Apple Watch's Side Button; the power of the menu will appear, but continue to hold the Side Button until the SOS countdown appears. (On the other hand, instead of holding the Side Button, you can just slide the emergency SOS control of the power of menu.)

By the end of the Apple Watch countdown, your local emergency Services will be called. (However, if you like to cancel the emergency call, release the button before the end of the countdown.

After the call, your emergency contacts that already set in the health app on your iPhone will automatically be notified, and even if the Location Services on your Watch is off, it will be temporarily activated

Philip Knoll

Chapter 19
Best Apple watches Applications

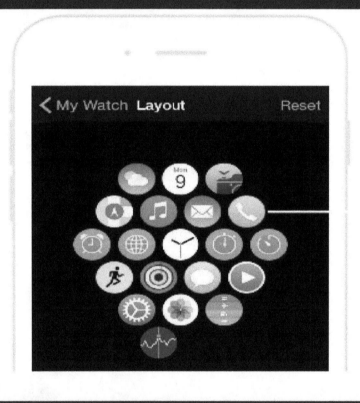

Touch and drag to move apps around.

These are the list of some selected applications for your Apple Watch.

Health and fitness Apps

Sleep++

One important thing that the Apple Watch doesn't yet accomplish is helping you figure out how well you're sleeping. In view of that, David Smith, developer of Pedometer++ a health and fitness apps, takes up that niche with his Sleep++ app, this app uses the Apple Watch's built-in sensors to track your hours of sleeping and waking. For using this app, just activate the app on your Apple Watch when you go to bed, again when you get up in the morning, and it'll provide you an idea of how restful your night's sleep has been.

Lose It!

The Apple Watch is attractive solid at helping you track your daily activity, but when it comes to fitness, the other end of the spectrum is tracking your food intake. That's where Lose It! Apples come in.

Apple Watch series 4

This App can give you an insight look at your current calorie budget for the whole day, your number of steps, your intake of nutrients and it can even know how you're doing for the week. For your good health, you can log your calories for your meals by force pressing on the main screen - no need to pull out your phone.

Pedometer

The pedometer is one of the fitness App. Fitness has e merged as one major selling point for the Apple

Philip Knoll

Watch. And as supportive as the three rings in the wa tch's Activity app might be, occasionally you just want hard data. Pedometer++ uses the accelerometer and sensors in both your phone and your Apple Watch to track how many steps you take every day. The app rewards you when you hit your goal with a shower of virtual confetti. It also has a built-in watch face barrier, so your step count and the distance you've walked is never more than a glance away.

Nike + Run Club

If you don't have one of those fancy Apple Watch Nike+ models you can still get the advantage of the company's workout app through the Nike+ Run Club app. It allows you to set goals for workout distance, duration, or speed, plus supporting voice over cues, the app has the ability to auto-pause when you stop running and running on treadmills. It also has bundles of a motivational aspect; focus you the weather for the day and allowing you to schedule an upcoming run, and displaying the current playlist of your music.

Philip Knoll

News

Overcast

Sometimes you may not feel like to listen to podcasts on your Apple Watch, but the Overcast app gives you control podcast playback from your phone, with controls to play and pause or jump back or forward 30 seconds. You can toggle Overcast's effects, like Voice Boost, Smart Speed and adjust playback speed. This app, in addition, shows you what's up next in your playback queue, as well as allowing you to generate new playlists on the fly.

Weather Apps

Carrot Weather

Apple Watch has a built-in Weather app which is fine as things go, but if you like to delve into something a bit more comprehensive (and a bit more detailed), Carrot Weather may be just what the meteorologist ordered. This App will give you the current conditions, a look at what the day holds, and even a little quip to keep things interesting. You can also toggle to multiple locations and there is a watch face complication, which includes both current conditions and temperature.

Philip Knoll

Utilities

Authy

Are you among the security conscious people? If yes, this App is right for you. You probably have many websites that use two-factor authentication.

This great app for maintenance track of all those two factor codes, and the Apple watch app let you reclaim t hem right from your wrist, instead of having to dig through your phone to find them. It has also come with a little time out bar that shows you how long you have before the code refreshes again.

Just Press Record

Another wonderful app, with another entry in the "qu ick notes" category, is the self-described Just Press Record by Open Planet Software. The main strength of this app is in letting you record swift audio notes. However, the app may not be enough for your podcast needs, but you can also record, playback, and save those audio notes, which are synce d via the cloud Drive to your iPhone. It can as well ad d transcriptions to short notes.

Philip Knoll

PCalc

If you don't want a calculator watch at a point?
TLA Systems's Pcalc is on apparently every Apple pl
atform, so an Apple watch edition is a natural fit.
This admired calculator not only offers basic math
operations, but also includes a built-in tip calculato
r and bill splitter, input by means of dictation or Scrib
ble, and it comes with handy conversion and mathemat
ical constant functions.

Navigation Apps

Citymapper

If you want to get around town, then Citymapper is an Apple Watch app for you. It handles much all forms of public transportation within the city, as well as giving options for biking, walking, and driving. There is swift access to saved destinations, as well as it is an ability to bring up nearby transit stops and spot when the next bus or train arrives.

Philip Knoll

Travel

Yelp

When you like to find a great nearby restaurant, coffee shop, or bar? The Yelp app here is the answer that will help you and to make it quick. You can scan through the listings of nearby businesses, and quickly glance at ratings and reviews, and pull up directions to the location via the Apple Watch's Maps app. With Yelp App on your Apple watch, you'll never go hungry again.

Apple Watch series 4

Lyft

Do you need a ride? The Lyft app can help you make that happen. It's a trouble-free and straightforward offering that lets you know how long it'll procure a car to get to your location. One of the pleasant features it o ffers over some other ride sharing apps is that it additi onally lets you enter a different pickup location through voice dictation.

Philip Knoll

Sports Apps

MLB.com At Bat

When you need the best number up-to-the-minute baseball scores without conceivably looking like you're checking the scores? MLB. com's At Bat app can assist by putting them right on your wrist. You know how to check the current scoreboard or skim via a list of teams to see how your favorites are doing on the baseball game.

Music Apps

Shazam

Shazam offers its excellent music-recognition skills to your Apple Watch very well. it is no longer that you have to fish out your phone fast enough to play "name that tune" just launch the Shazam app on your Apple Watch, tap the button and I'll listen to whatever's playing and it even shows you a match and lyrics likely.

Philip Knoll

Productivity Apps

Fantastical 2

This is among the best productivity apps for calendaring; there aren't many apps that will be aligned with Fantastical. Apple's built-in gift, Fantastical offers a scrollable list of imminent appointments for the week, detailed views of events, and to do items. You can also create a new event using dictation and get a quick glance at your upcoming events with your Apple watch face complication.

Drafts

If you want to give the impression of being captured with ideas when you're on the go? Just look no for Agi le Tortoise's Drafts. It is an Apple watch app which is ideal for those quick notes that bang into your head. When you launch the app, then tap the microph one icon to record a quick note, which will be transcrib ed into text and filed into your inbox. However, If you like, you can make use of the Advanced Capture options to insert an emoticon or use watch OS's Scribb le feature to enter your text letter by letter. In addition, you can even append, pre-pend, trash or archive individual notes in your inbox.

Reference Apps

Microsoft Translator

We may still be a far ways from the general translator of Star Trek, but apps like Microsoft Translator can still help a lot. With the Apple Watch version of this app, you can use dictation to speak a phrase and then have it translated into one of a number of languages. You will be able to see a text version of the translation, and still, in some cases hear it spoken aloud. Moreover, you can save frequently used snippets for future reference.

Finance Apps

Square Cash

This is another great App for finance, if you get it on your Apple watch. That is means you don't need to re ach for your wallet or your phone next time you need to send a friend some money. In its place, you can do it all from the Apple watch with the Square C ash app. Just tap on a contact from the list. Whichever you may like, either someone you've recently sent money to or anyone in your contact list. Just select *the amount of tapping the bill icons. You can tap more than one, so if you want to send $12, tap the $10 followed by the $1 twice. Then just send the money over and you're square cash it! This is great!.*

Chapter 20

Apple watches, best games.

Apple Watch games provide the crucial quick fix, allo wing you to solve puzzles. And hack away at enemies for a few minutes exclusive of going through the troubl e of pulling out your phone.

Favorites such as Trivia Crack make a perfect fit for t he Apple Watch's display, while text based adventure s such as SpyCatcher control the wearable computer to make you feel like you're a character in a sci-fi movie.

Pokémon Go

When you enormously, positively, must catch 'em all, sticking to your iPhone just won't suffice. Luckily, Pokémon Go provides an Apple Watch app that lets you carry out certain responsibilities, like incubating eggs that you've collected through physical activity. The more you walk or exercise, the closer those eggs get to hatching. You can as well visit Pokéstops, earn some cand *y, and be alerted to nearby Pokémon, without the need to pull out your phone.*

Komrad

Komrad is a text adventure game composes of Part War Games, part Cold War drama, where you're recruited to assist and retrieve secret codes from an antiquated Soviet AI program. You'll chat with the AI, selecting your conversational responses, which will dictate the course of the game. In addition, just in case you are inquisitive about the verisimilitude, the former Design Officer of IBM's Watson project created the game.

Philip Knoll

Pocket Bandit

Have you ever dreamed of committing a high stakes jewel heist? Pocket Bandit fulfills that yen, offering up a game in which you break into safes for the sweet, swe et loot. The catch? Here you must crack the combinati on locks by turning your Apple Watch's Digital Crow n, and then figure out the number by the haptic feedbac k you feel. Before the cops show up to take you away. Every safe you crack nets a differrrrent treasure, and t he game continues to add more as time goes on. It's br ainy, if not predominantly difficult, and, as a plus, requires no real lawbreaking.

Tiny Armies

A quick small strategy game, Tiny Armies puts you in charge of a number on it, tiny armies symbolized by blue squares with dots, trying to capture rival armies s ymbolized by red squares with xs. To do this, you swipe on blue armies to direct them, but must be careful they'll move in a straight line unless they hit an obstacle, like an impenetrable mountain, drowning la kes, or confusing forests. The board layouts   acquire *harder as you go, but it is a good game, that you can pick up and play when you have time for that.*

Field Day

Field Day is a good game that it does not take a green thumb to be successful. With this game, which sees yo u planting some crops and delivering orders, in fact, it requires the Apple Watch. As you go on, you'll engage more works and increase your farm to not just take in crops but animals as well. It's fascinating and cute, and a good game that gives way to scratch that itch to live your life as a typical farmer.

Rules!

The Apple Watch face display provides enough real estate for a first-class puzzle game, and Rules! is one of the best brain teasers game on the platform. The game starts cleanly, providing four numbered tiles and a basic rule, such as "tap in descending order." Nevertheless since a new rule gets added with every turn, you'll swiftly find yourself racking your noggin trying to follo

Philip Knoll

w them all. If you want to wake up your brain on the way to work, playing Rules! Is as good a way as any.

Lifeline

At the same time as a puzzle and word games work fi ne on the Apple Watch, Lifeline is the main model of a unique play experience that's best enjoyed on your Apple watch. The composes of a text-based adventure in which you help a stranded astronaut named Taylor ,Lifeline puts you in total control of the story by allowi ng you to decide how you respond to your new friend all through his dire journey.

Lifeline is playable on the iPhone and iPad, but playing it on your Watch makes it truly feel like you're exchanging messages with an astronaut by way of a futuristic transmitter. If you end, in short order, no worries: you can currently check out a number of sequels, including *Lifeline 2*, *Lifeline: Whiteout*, *Lifeline* and more.

Runeblade

The idea of playing a role-playing game on a tiny wristwatch may seem preposterous, but *Runeblade* pull s it off. This dungeon crawler keeps it basic, allowing y ou to hack away at a secure stream of mystical creatur es by just tapping your sword icon every few seconds. H owever, with rich, cartoon graphics; a perceptive upgrad e system; and a secure stream of new bosses and enviro nments to tackle, this miniature RPG is surprisingly alluring.

Trivia Crack

Trivia category-based quizzes have turned troves of iOS gamers into trivia addicts, and the game's Apple Watch counterpart makes it even easier to get your fix. Trivia Crack is a colorful spinni ng category wheel, cutely animated font, and fun questi ons, which touch on all from history to pop culture, Tr anslate elegantly to the Apple Watch's small screen. Y ou can still start a new game, right from your wrist.

Letter Zap

Letter Zap is one of the best letter-matching games that sacrifices little in its conversion to the Apple Wat ch. It's as chaste as word games get; you're tasked with untying as numerous words as likely in 30 seconds, w ith no special power-ups or unlockables to get in the way. Letter Zap's short-burst formula

Philip Knoll

makes it an ideal for Apple's Watch and the hunt of a high score will keep you playing for some time. There is a quick Apple-Watch-only challenge mode where you could have to form words while upholding your heartbeat under control.

Chapter 21
The Coolest Things that Apple

313

Philip Knoll

Watch Can Do

The Apple Watch is an amazingly capable device, but it still doesn't take you long to master the basics of what it can do. But, once you've got those basics down, it's time to change gears and try your hand at some of the smart but less obvious features that you can take advantage. This chapter will expose you to some of the coolest tips and tricks that your Apple Watch could do.

Go for a swim with your Apple watch

An Apple Watch was made with the water resistance capability if you have a natural inclination not to get your electronics wet. While the first version via series 4 was, water-resistant. Apple added the ability to submerge the watch up to 50 meters depth with the to i ts smart watch line. And that feature remain a part of the Series 3 and 4model, making them perfect for wor kouts at the local pool. However, always remember to use the Water Lock feature to get rid of any extra wat er from the speaker opening after your workout. Water

315

Lock kicks in automatically when you start a swimming workout and you can unlock the screen and clear out the water. When you're done by turning the digital crown. You must keep it in mind that if you take a swim in the ocean, you should perhaps rinse off the salt water with fresh water afterward.

Control your Apple TV and home theater.

Did you know that you can control an Apple TV with your Apple Watch? Or did you still remote slip between the couch cushions again? Do not mind that again. Your Apple Watch can control a number of home devices, while still leaves on your wrist.

For instance, if you have an Apple TV you can use t he Apple Watch's Remote app to swipe roughly the set top box's menus, start and pause playback, and more . Here you must get a Harmony Hub setup; you can run scripts from your Watch to turn on and off your home theater devices by using the IFTTT app on your Watch, despite the fact that, it will not yet let you do anything beyond that.

Talk to your car

If you've got a new automobile, your Apple Watch may give you ways to check on your car's status and in addition, you can even interact with it. Cars range f rom Mercedes Benz, BMW Porsche, VW and let you do a lot of things like lock and unlock your car's doors , honk the horn, checking battery levels on electric cars, and even assist you to find your parked car. Neverthel ess, If you've got an older car model or an aftermarket option from Viper you must include an app to let you lock, unlock, and start your car remotely.

Compete against your friends in fitness

Apple Watch can be used to measure yourself against your friends by turning on Activity Sharing. In the Activity app on iOS, go to the Sharing tab and tap the Plus (+) icon in the top right of your Watch to invite a friend to share their Activity info with you. Subsequently, you will be able to check their status in the Activity app on your Apple watch; you'll get notifications when they complete workouts.

Running without your iPhone

Speaking of working out, if you've got an Apple Watc h, you can lastly live the dream and leave your iPhone behind when you go for a run around the city. Because both models of the Apple watch have built-in GPS that can track your workout without needing to lug th at heavy phone in your hand or pocket. Plus, bring alo ng a pair of Bluetooth headphones for the trip and you can listen to music right off your Apple Watch as well. Moreover, Apple's own Workout app, you are capable of taking advantage of this in abundance of third-party apps like Nike+ Run Club and runkeeper.

Stream music without your phone

You'll require an Apple Watch Series 3 or 4 with LTE connectivity to pull off this feat, but it's one that will be a welcome aspect if you enjoy a little music add-on your run. Because the Series 3 model is able to connect to wireless networks on its own, you can stream songs without having your iPhone close at hand. An ideal for working out. And you're not immediate ly limited to, Apple Music and its ten Dollars-a-month streaming service. Apple too includes app called Radio with the Apple Smart Watch for streaming songs.

Unlock your Mac

Did you know your Apple watch can save you some ty ping difficulty? If you've got a Mac made within severa l years, your Apple Watch can be used to unlock the screen without having to enter any of your passwords. All you need to do is allow the ability on your Mac in System Preferences > Security & Privacy by checking the box next to Allow your Apple Watch to unlock y our Mac. Now, when you wake that Mac from sleep a nd you're wearing your Apple Watch, it should take c are of that wretched password business for you.

Scribble messages

There's no doubt, you know you can compose messages and emails on your Apple Watch through dictation, b ut did you also know that anywhere you can dictate a reply, you can also write one? A Scribble quality mass ages let you draw letters, numbers, and symbols on you r screen and have them automatically transformed into text. It's amazingly good, and very useful when you're in a place where perhaps you don't want to look similar to Dick Tracy talking to your Watch. When you want to enter a response, then tap the Scribble key and write away!.

Order food

One of the coolest things, that Apple watch can do. Whenever get so hungry that even taking your phone out look like a bridge too far? Providentially, you can order any food right from your Apple Watch, using a variety of apps. GrubHub lets you reorder recent favorites with just a couple taps or you can purposely order a pizza from Domino's or burritos from Chipotle.

Philip Knoll

Exposure to liquid

Apple Watch is water resistant but not waterproof. You may wear and use Apple Watch during exercise, exposure to sweat is acceptable, in the rain, and while washing your hands with water. If water splashes onto the watch, wipe it off with a nonabrasive, lint-free material. Do your best to minimize exposing Apple Watch to these substances like, Soap, detergent, acids or acidic foods, and any liquids other than fresh water, such as salt water, soapy water, pool water, perfume, i nsect repellent, lotions, sunscreen, oil, adhesive remover, hair dye, or solvents.

Submerging Apple Watch in a liquid is not recommended. Apple Watch has a water resistance ranking of I PX7 under IEC standard 60529. While the leather bands are not water resistant at all. Because water resistance is not a permanent, condition and an Apple smart watch cannot assume or resealed for water resistance.

Philip Knoll

The following may affect the water resistance of Apple Watch:

1. Dropping your Apple Watch or subjecting it to other impacts.

2. Submerging or sinking the watch in water for a long period.

3. Bathing or Swimming with Apple Watch.

4. Exposing Apple Watch to any pressurized water or high-velocity water, such as showering, water skiing, Wakeboarding, surfing, jet skiing, etc.

5. Wearing it in the sauna or steam room.

How to clean Apple Watch

Always keep your Apple Watch clean and dry. Clean and dry Apple smart Watch, the band, and your skin following workouts or profound sweating. Dry Apple Watch face and the band meticulously if they are exposed to fresh water.

Clean Apple Watch if exposed to everything that may cause stains, or other damage, such as dirt, sand, makeup, ink, soap, detergent, acid solution, or acidic f oods. Or when comes in contact with liquids other tha n water, including those that may lead to, skin irritati on like sweat, salt water, soapy water, pool water, perf ume, insect repellent, lotions, sunscreen, oil. Others are adhesive remover, hair dye, or solvents, etc. Despite the regular care, the Apple Watch and band colors may vary or fade over a period.

Turn off Apple Watch.

Press and hold the side button of your Watch, then drag the Power Off slider to the right.

Then depress the band release buttons and remove the band.

Wipe Apple Watch clean with a nonabrasive, lint-free cloth . You may also lightly dampen the cloth with fresh water.

Dry Apple Watch with a lint-free, nonabrasive cloth.

Apple Watch (gold) models benefit the most if you clean them frequently. Clean with a nonabrasive, lint free cloth to get rid of surface oil, perfumes, lotions, and other substances, particularly before storing Apple Watch.

Philip Knoll

These things not recommended in the care of your Apple Smart Watch:

1. Do not clean Apple watch at the same time as its charging.

2. Do not dry Apple Watch, the bands using an external heat source like a hair dryer.

3. Do not use chemical cleaning products or compressed air when cleaning your Apple Watch.

The front of Apple Watch is made by Ion-X glass or sapphire crystal, each with a fingerprint-resistant oleophobic which is oil repellent coating substances. This coating material wears over time with normal usage. Cleaning products and abrasive substances will further diminish the coating, and may probably scratch the glass or the sapphire crystal.

Using buttons, Digital Crown, connectors, and ports

You should never apply excessive pressure to a button or the Digital Crown on Apple Watch, or to force a charging connector into its port, for the reason that, this may cause damage that is not covered under the company warranty. Take note that if the connector and port don't join with reasonable ease, most likely they don't match. Check for any obstruction and make sure that *the connector matches the port and that you have placed the connector correctly in relation to the port.*

Some certain usage patterns can be a factor in the fraying or breaking of cables. The cable attached to a charging component, like any other metal cable, is subject to becoming brittle or weak if repetitively bent in the same spot. This will be prevented by gentle curves instead of angles in the cable. On a regular bas is, inspect the cable and connector for any kinks, brea ks, bends, or any damage. In case you find any such damage, discontinue use of the cable.

Apple Watch series 4

It is normal after regular use the lightning connector to USB cable can get discoloration. Extreme dirt, debris , and exposure to moisture may cause discoloration. If your lightning, cable or connector become so warm during use or if Apple Watch won't charge, disconnect the cable from the power adapter and clean the lightning connector with a non-corrosive, dry, lint-free cloth. You should not use liquids or cleaning agent when cleaning the Lightning connector.

Philip Knoll

Magnetic charging cable and magnetic ch arging case

The Apple Watch magnetic charging cable and magne tic charging case discoloration of the charging surface may occur after regular use due to dirt and debris that come in contact with the magnetic surface. This is com mon. Cleaning the magnetic charging surface may redu ce, or prevent, that discoloration, and will help to preve nt damage to your charger and Apple smart Watch. if you want to clean the charging surface, disconnect the c harger from both Apple Watch and the power adapter outlets and wipe with a damp, nonabrasive lint-free cloth.

Always dry it with a nonabrasive, lint free cloth before charging again. This also not requires using cleaning chemical agent when cleaning the charging surface.

Apple Watch optimum ambient temperature

Apple Watch operating temperature is designed to work best in ambient temperatures between 0° and 35 °C and be stored in temperatures between -20° and 45° C. Apple Watch can be spoiled and battery l ife reduced if stored or operated outside of these ambien *t temperature ranges. Avoid exposing your Apple Wa tch to remarkable changes in temperature or humidity. When the interior temperature of Apple smart Watch exceeds normal operating temperatures (for instance, i n extremely hot weather or in direct sunlight for long p eriod of time), you may likely experience the following as the Apple smart operating capabilities att empt to regulate its temperature:*

Charging may possibly slow or stop.

1. The Apple display may dim.

2. A temperature-warning screen icon may appear.

3. Certain data transfer may be paused or delayed.

4. Some of Apple apps may close.

It is very important to know that, you may not be able to use Apple Watch whereas the temperature-warning screen is displayed. Because, if Apple Watch can't regulate its internal ambient temperature, it usually goes into power reserve or a deep sleep mode until it cools down. When this problem occurs, move your Apple smart Watch to a cooler location out of direct sunlight or hot car and wait a few minutes before trying to use it again.

Philip Knoll

It is very essential to keep key cards and credit cards a way from Apple Watch, the bands, the Apple Watch magnetic charging cable, and the Apple Watch magnetic charging case.

Chapter 22

BEST APPLE WATCH BANDS

Who cares that someone has a solid gold Apple Watch band?. Now there are several fashionable options available — even some you can customize — your personal style will come shining through when you wear your new smartwatch, you won't need to spend $15,000 on the precious metal. These simple, well-designed, and chic watch band designs range from $16.00 to $250, and since Apple makes it easy to slide in and out new bands, you can have one to match any outfit.

Philip Knoll

APPLE MILANESE LOOP

The brand Milanese Loop band from Apple epitomizes modern swank while still evoking 19th-century Italian style. The stainless-steel mesh wraps all the way around your wrist to magnetically close without any fumbling over clasps. Because it's substant ially adjustable, this band should fit any wrist to perfection.

APPLE WATCH LEATHER LOOP

Add a few Italian luxuries to your Apple Watch with the company's $148 leather loop band. The band's Venezia leather has a unique, distressed look, and it *comes in 4 muted-yet-chic colors: blue, black, brown and taupe. It has a magnetic closure for easy fastening and removing the Apple watch, and the closure is adjustable, so you can make it as tight if you wish or as loose as you want.*

APPLE WATCH WOVEN NYLON BAND

This woven nylon is durable yet still stylish, Apple's own nylon bands are made from more than 500 colorful threads woven together in 4 layers for a fabric-like feel. The band comes in Light Pink/Midnight Blue, Yellow/Light

Gray, Space Orange or Anthracite, Toasted Coffee or Caramel and Nav Tahoe Blue.

APPLE MODERN BUCKLE

For the true Apple fan, the Midnight Blue Modern Buckle is a very stylish selection. The top-grain leather looks luxurious, while the two-piece magnetic closure of the buckle is extremely refined. The leather strap comes in black, brown, or pink as well, but the deep blue offers a subtle hint of cultivated style.

COACH APPLE WATCH STUDS LEATHER STRAP

Bring your Apple Watch to look back down to earth a bit with this Western-style, soft leather strap dotted with lacquered studs. Besides the pictured ginger version, the band comes in black, with both versions offering studs in olive, titanium and a pearly white. Designed solely for women, this Coach band is sized only for the 38 mm Apple Watch.

Philip Knoll

CASETIFY CUSTOMIZE APPLE WATCH BAND

Most the do-it-yourselfers know the value of making amazing for themselves. With Casetify's Customized Apple Watch Band, you can do just that. Through the site, you can upload images, use emoji or connect to your Instagram or Facebook account to grab photos to place on the watchband. Then, you can add one of 8 photo filters, such as sepia, to give the 6 pictures you choose a similar look.

MONOWEAR NYLON OLIVE BAND WITH CHROME LOOPS

This Monowear Nylon Olive Band with Chrome Loops works best with the stainless-steel or silver-aluminum watch faces. The loops keep the surplus band from flapping around, while the rugged nylon material adds an air of funk and independence to the popular smartwatch.

MONOWEAR BLACK METAL

While indistinctly reminiscent of the Apple Link Brac elet, the Monowear Black Metal is just a bit snazzier. Its stainless-steel structure is swathed in a matte black

Philip Knoll

color. This band is also available in either 38 mm or 42 mm for the Watch Sport, Watch Edition or base Watch. It can be customized to adapt flawlessly with Apple's stainless-steel, aluminum or space-gray watch faces.

ETSY MINIMALIST AND ZEN WATCH STRAP

This is for those who love the refined look of leather and prefer a simple design, the Etsy Minimalist and Zen Watch Strap may be just the answer. Available in 38 mm or 42 mm, it's made of vegetable-tanned *leather that will probably fade from yellow to brown over time; applying neatsfoot oil or mink oil will speed up this change. You can select a golden- or silver-Colore brass stud clasp.*

How to care Apple Watchband

It is advisable to use only Apple-branded or Apple authorized bands.
Clean the bands, remove the band from Apple Watch prior to cleaning.

Nevertheless, for the leather part of the bands, wipe th em clean with a nonabrasive, lint free cloth, lightly da mpened with water. After cleaning, allow the band air dry thoroughly before re-attaching it back to Apple Watch. You should not store leather bands in direct su nlight, at very high temperatures, or in high humidity. Furthermore, don't soak leather bands in fresh water. The leather bands are not water resistant.

For other bands and clasps, wipe them clean with a nonabrasive, lint-free cloth, lightly dampened with water. Dry the band thoroughly with a nonabrasive, lint-free cloth before reattaching it back.

How to remove, change, and fasten bands

In this part, you will learn the general instructions for removing,
changing, and fastening bands. All the time ensure that you're replacing a band with a similar one of the same size. The bands are sized according to the size of Apple smart Watch and should not be just used interchangeably. Some band styles made specifically for a particular size Apple smart Watch only.

To change bands

Press the band release button on your Apple Watch, slide the band across to remove it, and then slide the new band. Never force a new band into the it's slot. However, if you're having difficulty removing or inserting a band, then press the band release button again.

The band release button

Fasten a band. For a greater performance, Apple smart Watch should fit closely on your wrist. The back of Apple Watch needs a good skin contact for features

Apple Watch series 4

Like wrist detection, haptic notifications, and the heart rate sensor. It is also another trick for wearing Apple smart Watch with the right fit-not too tight, not too loose, and with enough room for your skin to breathe. This may keep you more comfortable and let the sensors do their work. At times, you may like to tighten Apple Watch for your workouts, and then loosen the band when you're done. In addition, the device sensors will work only when you wear the Watch on the top of your wrist.

Philip Knoll

Conclusions

Thank you again for downloading this book!

I hope you have enjoyed this book and we hope that you are going to enjoy your smart watch maximally and efficiently. Finally, please take the time to share y our thoughts and post a review on Amazon. It would greatly appreciate!

Thank you and good luck!

About the author

Philip Knoll *is CEO of Graw-Hill, the publishing company that published several IT books. He worked at Inte-route, Europe's largest voice and data network provider. Before Inte-route, he was working as a senior network engineer for Globtel Internet, a signif icant Internet and Telephony Services Provider to the market. He has been working with Linux for more than 10 years putting a strong accent on security for protecting vital data from hackers and ensuring goo* d quality services for internet customers. Moving to Vo IP services he had to focuseven more on security as sens itive billing data is most often stored on servers with pu blic IP addresses. He has been studying QoS impleme ntations on Linux to build different types of services for IP customers and also to deliver good quality for th em and for VoIP over the public Internet.Philip has a lso been programming educational software's with Perl, PHP, and Smarty for over 7 years mostly developing in-house management interfaces for IP and VoIP services.

Apple Watch series 4

Philip Knoll

Bonus for buying this book.

The link; to download your book

https://techguideblog.net/free-ebook-60-minutes-apple-watch-guide/

Our website is http//www.techguideblog.net

You should check it out and let me know what you think. I keep a blog there for our efficient interaction. I like to invite you follow my journey, by signing up *my free newsletter. If you subscribed youll get free copy of my books.mp3, pdf files, and tutorials*

The list of my favorite online tools, plus notification of free future kindles book and offers. Pleases, if you're interested signup.

Philip Knoll

Preview of another books

Book 1

Apple Watch

2018 Apple user guide including tips and tricks

(Apple smart Watch)

Apple Watch series 4

Introduction

This might not be in the main area of being cool but it was appealing marvelous. Last week I went out to start my generator and I gave it a big ole pull and accidentally off flies my Apple Watch Series 3 from my wrist, it flew through the air about 20 yards and fell into my thousand liters water tank which was actually the lid off. Nevertheless, there is my five-month old Apple watch in the bottom of a thousand liters of water. But Mind you my tank is about four feet tall and about six feet wide with an opening of about 15 inches, my first contemplation was, "waterproofing tech don't fail." After about 25 minutes of fishing around with a bait of magnet, I pulled my Apple Watch out of its soggy resting lair and it was just fine and working perfectly.

Why do you need Apple Watch?

There are so many reasons for using Apple Watch because it comes with different amazing functionality. When using the Apple Watch, it can monitor your heart rate and mind you your heart rate is the most essential among the vital sign of your life. The Apple Watch uses photoplethysmography technology (PPG) which uses the green LED lights to measure your heart rates. To determine a user's heart rate, the Apple watch flashes green light from the LEDs at the skin of user's and detects the amount of this light that is absorbed by the red pigment of your blood. The following are some of the reasons why you need an Apple Watch.

Why should we use Apple watch?

1. Easy access to your phone information and including all your notifications

2. Your watch can easily respond to the text quickly and phone calls can be simply be taken from your wrist with the feeling of satisfaction

3. *The Apple watch has an excellent fitness tracker/companion and that can be used for all your workout needs and exercise*

4. *The watch also came with preinstalled applications that are well designed and functional*

5. *The new Series 2 and 3 is absolutely waterproof so you can wear the watch almost everywhere*

6. *It has good battery life much better it was advertised*

Generation of Apple watches

Generally speaking, Apple Watch was initially released in April 2015 as the first generation Apple Watch,

Apple Watch series 4

As of October 2017, four generations, and four series of Apple Watch have been released. The series in bold are currently produced:

1. Apple Watch from 2015 to 2016

2. Apple Watch Series 1 from 2016 to present

3. Apple Watch Series 2 from 2016 to 2017

4. Apple Watch Series 3 from 2017– 2018

5. Apple watches series 4 from Nov 2018 to date

The Apple Watch Series 2 and Series 3 models are further divided into four "Apple Watch collection":

Philip Knoll

- *Apple Watch,*

- *Apple Watch Nike+*

- *Apple Watch Hemes*

- *Apple Watch Edition.*

The only differences between these Apple smart Watch collections are differentiated solely by combinations of their cases, bands, and exclusive watch faces. The first collection Apple Watch comes with either aluminum or stainless steel cases or different watch bands; the second collection Apple Watch Nike+ utilizes aluminum

Apple Watch series 4

cases and special types of sport band; the third collection of Apple Watch Hemes comes with stainless steel cases and Hemes watch bands; while the fourth collection of Apple smart Watch Edition comes with ceramic versions cases.

However, for the Apple Watch Series 1 models they only come with aluminum cases and sports bands. Finally, Apple smart Watch Series 3 models are sold with a modification that allows for cellular LTE capability.

All models come in either 38- or 42-millimeter body, with the 42 mm size having a little larger screen and battery. However, all Apple Watch models have various color and band style. Apple-made bands consist of colored sports bands, sports loop, woven nylon band, classic buckle, modern buckle, leather loop, Milanese loop, and a link bracelet.

Apple Watch series 4

www.amazon.com/dp/B07FS33G5Y

Philip Knoll

Book 2

APPLE WATCH

SERIE 4 SECRETS GUIDE

The 24 hours complete User guide to master the new series 4 Watch Os 5.1.2 with question and answers

(Get two free books bonus for purchasing this book)

368

Apple Watch series 4

Are you an owner of an Apple Smart Watch? If so, you would be well aware of how popular they are right now, especially considering that it's just like having your phone complete with its list of essential functions strapped to your wrist at all times.

For fans of Apple products, an Apple watch may be the perfect investment if you're looking to create a more personalized user experience. It's also a far more convenient way to make calls and look up other information quickly and easily.

Philip Knoll

Once you've invested a lot of money in a Smart Watch, why not optimize it and make full use of all its functions?

In truth, there are a lot of secrets to optimizing your Apple Smart Watch experience. How do you do it, you ask? It's quite simple and only a technical matter.

However, how do you use it? What is the best way to make the most of your device? How do you use the basic and extended functions of the Watch? You're about to find out!

With this user manual, you can discover everything you need to know about an Apple Smart Watch — all within two hours. You will also learn simplified tips and tricks that will have you using your Smart Watch like a pro in no time.

Here is a preview of what you'll learn:

- ✓ *The doctor on your wrist (Apple Watch Series 4*
- ✓ *s Apple Watch Series 4 100% perfect?*
- ✓ **The word of wisdom**

Philip Knoll

✓ *Apple watch series 4 the latest version*

✓ *101 questions professionally answers about apple watch*

✓ *Smartwatch buying guide*

✓ *How apple design Apple watch*

✓ *Why do you need Apple Watch*

✓ *What we observed on Apple series 4*

✓ *The sensor of the Apple Watch Series 4*

✓ *Apple Watch troubleshooting*

✓ *Apple watches questions and answers*

✓ *How to clean Apple Watch*

✓ *Best Apple watches Applications*

✓ ***Apps and Watch Faces***
✓ ***What we are expecting on Apple watch series 5***

And much more……

When it comes to the Apple Watch, the system and interface may seem new and unfamiliar, and you may feel that you can't understand how to use it – but that's perfectly alright, because this book will guide you through the process of getting to know and completely mastering your Apple Watch.

Philip Knoll

By the end of this book, you will be able to use the watch successfully not only in terms of the basic functions, but you will also get to know a lot of new and exciting tips and tricks.

With new generations coming out, learning more about it is essential so you can use your Apple Smart Watch successfully and keep up with the evolution of the device. Don't get left behind!

Apple Watch series 4

Get your copy of "Apple Watch secrets guide" by scrolling up and clicking "Buy Now With 1-Click" button.

Philip Knoll

Book 3

Apple Watch ECG

The ultimate ECG Interpretation's Guide

How to analyze Apple watch ECG like a Professional

What you are about to read in this book may be good for your health and it can even save your life. The Apple watch ECG, the ultimate ECG Interpretation Guide, How to analyze Apple watch ECG like a Professional Would arm you with knowledge like a professional using Apple watch for arrhythmias detection.

Apple Watch series 4

Apple sponsored a bilateral multicenter study to evaluate and validate the ability of the ECG app to generate an ECG waveform like a lead 1 ECG from the standard 12-lead ECG and utilize a rhythm classification algorithm to use the single-lead ECG that would classify heart rhythm into normal sinus rhythm and atrial fibrillation.

With watch OS 5.1.2, Apple watch series 1 and later version are capable of identifying period of irregular pulse suggestive of atrial fibrillation using photoplethysmo graph (PPG) signals combined algorithm. In addition to this PPG-based identification algorithm, Apple watch series 4 has electrical heart sensor that. When using the ECG app, enable the generation and analysis of an ECG similar to lead 1 of the standard ECG.

The truth is, there is a lot of secret that you need to know about your Apple Watch ECG app. And how to do it, it quite easy and simple.

Nevertheless, how do you use it? What's the best way to get the most out of this? How do you use this on your watch? Well, you're about to find out. Everything that you need to know about the Apple watch ECG functions are included in *this; along with simplified tips and tricks to better help you understand how to use this. By the end of this, yo u'll know exactly how to use the Apple Watch ECG perfectly.*

Here is a preview of what you'll learn:

- *The Doctor on Your Wrist*
- *How Apple watch is saving Lives*
- *What you need to know about the ECG*

- *General functions of ECG*

- *How the ECG App Works*

Philip Knoll

- *Is It Accurate?*
- *Apple Watch for heart disease detection*
- *Preclinical development test*
- *Clinical Validation from Apple Heart Study*
- *Apple watch ECG Description*
- *ECG determination on Apple Watch*
- *And much more..!*

With the Apple Watch, it might seem like a newer system that you don't understand how to use. That's fine, it's totally okay. However, with this book, you'll be able to learn everything that you need to know about the Apple Watch ECG app, and how to better master it. You'll be able to use this App watch in a successful way and know how to not just do all of the basic functions, but also how to master other cool tips and tricks as well. With new generations of this coming out, it's worth learning more about, so that you can use this successfully.

Get *your copy of "Apple Watch ECG"* **by scrollingup and clicking "Buy Now With 1-Click" button**.

Philip Knoll

 *2 books Bonus for buying this book.*

The link; to download your book

https://techguideblog.net/free-ebook-60-minutes-apple-watch-guide/

Our website is http//www.techguideblog.net

You should check it out and let me know what you think. I keep a blog there for our efficient interaction.

I like to invite you follow my journey, by signing up my free newsletter. If you subscribed youll get free copy of my books.mp3, pdf files, and tutorials

The list of my favorite online tools, plus notification of free future kindles book and offers. Pleases, if you're interested signup.

Thank you.